Electric Steamer RECIPE BOOK

Delicious and Nutritious Recipes for Your Electric Steamer

DOROTHY R. JACKSON

COPYRIGHT

Copyright © by Dorothy R. Jackson All rights reserved. No part of this book may be reproduced, distributed, or transmitted in any form or by any means, including photocopying, recording, or other electronic or mechanical methods, without the prior written permission of the publisher, except in the case of brief quotations embodied in critical reviews and certain other noncommercial uses permitted by copyright law.

TABLE OF CONTENTS

INTRODUCTION 9
HOW TO USE ELECTRIC STEAMER FOR COOKING? 11
WHO NEED ELECTRIC STEAMER FOR COOKING? 13
BREAKFAST DELIGHTS 15

1. Tropical Steamed Oatmeal 15
2. Spiced Chickpea Scramble Bowls 16
3. Rainbow Veggie Frittata Stacks 17
4. Honey-Mustard Glazed Salmon 18
5. Rainbow Dumpling Delight 19
6. Steamed Oatmeal with Berries and Chia Seeds 21
7. Asian-Style Steamed Buns with Eggs 22
8. Savory Salmon Steam Buns 24
9. Spinach and Feta Frittata Cups 26
10. Steamed Asparagus and Poached Egg Croissants 27
11. Steamed Breakfast Burrito Bowls 28
12. Poached Eggs Florentine 29

SNACKS AND APPETIZERS 30

13. Steamed Shrimp and Asparagus Parcels 30
14. Spicy Steamed Mussels 31
15. Vegetable Shumai 32
16. Vegetable and Corn Dumplings 33
17. Vegetable Gyoza Potstickers 35
18. Steamed Edamame and Tofu Spring Rolls 37
19. Steamed Chicken & Broccoli Buns 38
20. Steamed Chicken Potstickers 40
21. Steamed Chicken and Mushroom Shu Mai 42
22. Steamed Fish Bao 43
23. Steamed Edamame Pods 44
24. Dim Sum Siu Mai (Pork Dumplings) 45

VEGETABLES 46

25. Curried Chickpea and Veggie Bowls 46
26. Asian Vegetable Spring Rolls 48
27. Spicy Asian Broccoli 49
28. Lemon-Garlic Brussels Sprouts 50
29. Honey-Sriracha Cauliflower Bites 51
30. Garlic Herb Green Beans 52
31. Mediterranean Stuffed Peppers 53
32. Rainbow Veggie Medley 54
33. Garlic Scape and Tomato Bruschetta 55
34. Honey Glazed Carrots 56
35. Roasted Root Vegetable Medley 57
36. Roasted Butternut Squash with Sage 58

HEALTHY TWISTS 59

    37. Rainbow Veggie Spring Rolls 59
    38. Korean-Inspired Steamed Chicken Wraps 60
    39. Steamed Chicken and Vegetable Pad Thai 61
    40. Spicy Tofu and Edamame Lettuce Wraps 63
    41. Salmon with Lemony Asparagus and Quinoa 65
    42. Spicy Chipotle Black Bean Burgers 66
    43. Curried Carrot and Chickpea Fritters 67
    44. Mango and Black Bean Salsa Verde 68
    45. Lentil and Sweet Potato Shepherd's Pie 69
    46. Steamed Shrimp Scampi with Zucchini Noodles 70
    47. Spicy Sweet Potato and Black Bean Tacos 71
    48. Turmeric Cauliflower Rice Buddha Bowl 72

SIDE DISHES 74

    49. Garlic Herb Green Beans 74
    50. Garlic Scape and Tomato Bruschetta 75
    51. Honey-Glazed Carrots with Orange Zest 75
    52. Honey-Sriracha Glazed Brussels Sprouts 76
    53. Honey Glazed Carrots with Pecans 77
    54. Mediterranean Stuffed Peppers 78
    55. Steamed Artichokes with Lemon Butter Dip 79
    56. Rainbow Veggie Medley with Quinoa 80
    57. Steamed Asparagus with Balsamic Glaze 81
    58. Steamed Sugar Snap Peas with Sesame Oil 82
    59. Asian Steamed Broccoli with Sesame Sauce 83
    60. Spicy Asian Edamame Pods 84

FISH & SEAFOOD 85

    61. New England-Style Steamed Lobster Tails 85
    62. Spicy Cajun Shrimp Boil 86
    63. Steamed Scallops with Lemon Butter Sauce 87
    64. Asian-Style Steamed Fish in Banana Leaves 88
    65. Steamed Lemongrass Salmon with Coconut Rice 89
    66. Hawaiian Steamed Mahi Mahi with Mango Salsa 90
    67. Steamed Tilapia with Tropical Fruit Salsa 91
    68. Steamed Clams with Chorizo and White Wine 92
    69. Cantonese Steamed Fish with Soy Sauce and Ginger 93
    70. Vietnamese Steamed Fish with Nuoc Cham Sauce 94
    71. Steamed Mussels with Garlic White Wine Broth 95
    72. Thai Steamed Fish Cakes with Sweet Chili Sauce 96

POULTRY 97

    73. Spicy Garlic Ginger Chicken 97
    74. Asian-Style Chicken Lettuce Wraps 98
    75. Chicken and Vegetable Skewers 99
    76. Steamed Chicken and Dumplings 100
    77. Steamed Chicken and Cornbread Stuffing 101

78. Honey Mustard Glazed Chicken Drumsticks 102
79. Steamed Chicken and Vegetable Medley 103
80. Herb-Crusted Steamed Chicken Breasts 104
81. Lemon Garlic Chicken Wings 105
82. Chicken and Quinoa Stuffed Peppers 106
83. Chicken and Chorizo Sausage Stew 108
84. Poached Chicken Salad 109

INTERNATIONAL DISHES 110

85. Brazilian Coxinha Chicken Croquettes 110
86. Korean Mandu Dumplings with Kimchi Dip 112
87. Moroccan Chicken Msemen with Honey Butter 113
88. Italian Steamed Mussels with Garlic 114
89. Vietnamese Steamed Banh Beo Rice Cakes 115
90. Peruvian Steamed Aji de Gallina Chicken Stew 116
91. Greek Steamed Dolmadakia Grape Leaves 117
92. Mexican Steamed Tamales with Salsa Verde 119
93. German Potato Dumplings 121
94. Japanese Gyoza Potstickers 122
95. Chinese Har Gow Shrimp Dumplings 124
96. Ethiopian Misir Wot Lentil Stew 126

MAIN COURSES 127

97. Steamed Salmon with Lemon & Herbs 127
98. Chicken & Chorizo Sausage Stew 128
99. Steamed Chicken Pot Pie Filling 129
100. Steamed Shrimp & Grits 130
101. Lemon Garlic Chicken Breasts 131
102. Spicy Black Bean Burgers 132
103. Steamed Fish with Ginger & Soy Sauce 133
104. Moroccan Chickpea & Sweet Potato Tagine 134
105. Stuffed Peppers with Quinoa & Veggies 135
106. Steamed Pork Buns with Hoisin Sauce 136
107. Korean Bulgogi Beef 138
108. Stuffed Acorn Squash with Quinoa 139

DESSERTS & SWEET ENDINGS 140

109. Steamed Chocolate Cherry Brownies 140
110. Tropical Fruit Steamed Dumplings 141
111. Raspberry and Almond Steamed Crumble 142
112. Spiced Steamed Pears with Vanilla Sauce 143
113. Steamed Banana Bread with Chocolate Chunks 144
114. Steamed Chocolate Peanut Butter Bars 146
115. Steamed Sticky Fig Pudding 147
116. Gingerbread Pear Steamed Pudding 148
117. Steamed Chocolate Pudding Cakes 150
118. Sticky Toffee Steamed Buns 151
119. Steamed Pumpkin Spice Cake with Maple Glaze 152
120. Steamed Apple Crisp with Oat Crumble 153

Introduction

Welcome to the Electric Steamer Recipe Book, a culinary companion designed to elevate your cooking experience with the convenience and health benefits of steam cooking. Authored by Dorothy R. Jackson, this comprehensive collection of recipes offers a diverse array of dishes spanning from breakfast delights to satisfying desserts.

In today's fast-paced world, where time is a precious commodity and health is paramount, the electric steamer emerges as a hero in the kitchen. Its simple yet efficient design allows for the retention of nutrients and flavors in your meals, making it an indispensable tool for the modern home cook.

Within these pages, you will discover a plethora of mouthwatering recipes carefully crafted to showcase the versatility of your electric steamer. From hearty breakfast options to delectable desserts, each recipe has been thoughtfully curated to provide not only delicious meals but also nourishing goodness for you and your loved ones.

Explore the chapters dedicated to wholesome vegetables, innovative healthy twists, and tantalizing international dishes that will transport your taste buds to far-flung culinary destinations. Indulge in succulent fish and seafood creations, flavorful poultry dishes, and a variety of side dishes that perfectly complement any main course.

Whether you're a seasoned chef looking to expand your repertoire or a novice cook seeking inspiration, the Electric Steamer Recipe Book has something for everyone. Join us on a culinary journey where flavor meets convenience and health is never compromised. Get ready to embark on a delicious adventure that will transform the way you cook with your electric steamer.

How to use Electric Steamer for cooking?

Using an electric steamer for cooking is a simple and convenient way to prepare a wide range of dishes while retaining their nutrients and flavors. Here's a step-by-step guide on how to use an electric steamer for cooking:

Prepare the Steamer:
Ensure that your electric steamer is clean and in good working condition.
Fill the water reservoir with the appropriate amount of water according to the manufacturer's instructions. There is often a marked maximum level indicating how much water to add.

Assemble the Steamer Baskets:
Depending on your electric steamer model, assemble the steamer baskets or trays. Make sure they fit securely in the steamer base.

Preheat the Steamer (if necessary):
Some electric steamers require preheating, while others do not. Follow the manufacturer's instructions regarding preheating if applicable.

Prepare Ingredients:
Wash and prepare the ingredients you plan to steam. This may include vegetables, fish, poultry, grains, or dumplings, depending on your recipe.

Seasoning (optional):
Season your ingredients with herbs, spices, sauces, or marinades as desired before placing them in the steamer baskets. This adds flavor to your dishes.

Arrange Ingredients in Steamer Baskets:
Place the prepared ingredients evenly in the steamer baskets or trays. Be careful not to overcrowd them to ensure even cooking.

Set Cooking Time and Temperature:
Depending on your recipe or the type of food you are cooking, set the desired cooking time and temperature on the steamer control panel. Refer to the user manual for specific instructions.

Start Cooking:
Once you have set the cooking time and temperature, start the steamer. The steamer will generate steam, which will cook the ingredients in the baskets.

Monitor Cooking Progress:
Keep an eye on the cooking progress, especially during the first few minutes. Adjust the cooking time or temperature if necessary.

Check for Doneness:
Carefully open the steamer lid towards the end of the cooking time to check if the ingredients are cooked to your liking. Use a fork or knife to test for tenderness.

Serve or Store:
Once the ingredients are cooked to perfection, carefully remove them from the steamer using tongs or a spatula.
Serve your delicious steamed dishes immediately, or store them in a covered dish to keep warm until serving.

Cleaning:
After use, allow the electric steamer to cool down completely before cleaning.
Disassemble the steamer baskets or trays and wash them with warm, soapy water. Wipe down the base and other components as necessary.
Follow the manufacturer's instructions for cleaning and maintenance to ensure the longevity of your electric steamer.
By following these steps, you can easily use your electric steamer to cook a variety of dishes with minimal effort and maximum flavor. Experiment with different ingredients and recipes to discover new culinary delights.

Who need Electric Steamer for cooking?

Electric steamers are versatile kitchen appliances that can benefit a wide range of people, including:

Health-conscious individuals: Electric steamers are ideal for those who prioritize healthy cooking. Steaming helps retain nutrients in food better than other cooking methods like boiling or frying.
Busy professionals: People with hectic schedules who still want to enjoy home-cooked meals can benefit from electric steamers. They offer a convenient way to prepare meals with minimal effort and supervision.

Parents: Electric steamers are great for families, especially parents of young children. They can easily steam vegetables, meats, and other nutritious ingredients for homemade baby food or family meals.

Fitness enthusiasts: Individuals focused on maintaining a balanced diet and controlling portion sizes can use electric steamers to prepare lean proteins, vegetables, and grains without added oils or fats.

Vegetarians and vegans: Electric steamers provide an excellent way to cook a variety of vegetables, grains, and plant-based proteins, allowing vegetarians and vegans to create flavorful and nutritious meals.

Cooking novices: Beginners in the kitchen who are still learning their way around cooking techniques can benefit from the simplicity of electric steamers. They are easy to use and require minimal culinary skills.

Elderly individuals: Electric steamers offer a safe and simple cooking method for older adults who may have mobility issues or difficulty standing for long periods. Steaming also produces softer textures, which can be easier to chew and digest.

People with dietary restrictions: Those with dietary restrictions or food allergies can appreciate the versatility of electric steamers. They can easily control the ingredients and seasonings used in their meals to accommodate their specific dietary needs.

Small apartment dwellers: Individuals living in small apartments or dorm rooms with limited kitchen space can benefit from the compact size and versatility of electric steamers, which can often serve multiple cooking functions in one appliance.

Environmentally conscious individuals: Electric steamers are an eco-friendly cooking option since they use minimal water and energy compared to traditional cooking methods. They also produce less waste since no oils or fats are needed for cooking.

Overall, electric steamers can be a valuable addition to any kitchen, catering to a diverse range of dietary preferences, lifestyles, and cooking abilities.

BREAKFAST DELIGHTS

1. TROPICAL STEAMED OATMEAL

Prep Time: 5 minutes | Cook Time: 20 minutes

Total Time: 25 minutes | Serving: 1

Ingredients

- 1/2 cup of rolled oats
- 1 cup of water or milk
- Pinch of salt
- Optional: Tropical fruits like mango, pineapple, papaya, banana (fresh or frozen)
- Optional: Tropical spices like ground ginger, cinnamon, nutmeg, cardamom
- Optional: Toppings like toasted coconut flakes, chopped nuts, seeds, honey, maple syrup

Instructions

1. Put the oats, water or milk, and salt in the basket of your electric steamer.
2. Cut up any tropical fruits you want to use and add them.
3. If you want to, sprinkle with your favorite tropical spices.
4. Follow the cooking time directions that came with your steamer. Aim for 20 minutes for rolled oats. If you want quick oats, you may need more steamer power.
5. Toast your toppings (if you want) while the oatmeal cooks.
6. Use a fork to fluff the oatmeal after it's done cooking.
7. Put oatmeal into bowls and add any toppings you like on top of them. Have fun!

2. SPICED CHICKPEA SCRAMBLE BOWLS

Prep Time: 10 minutes | Cook Time: 20 minutes

Total Time: 30 minutes | Serving: 2

Ingredients

- 1/2 tsp ground turmeric
- 1/2 cup of chopped red bell pepper
- 1 can (15 ounce) chickpeas, drained and rinsed
- 1 clove garlic, minced
- 1/4 tsp ground cumin
- 1/4 cup of chopped onion
- 1/4 tsp chili powder
- 1 tbsp olive oil
- Pinch of smoked paprika
- Salt and pepper to taste
- 1/4 cup of chopped fresh cilantro (optional)
- 1/2 cup of cherry tomatoes, halved (optional)
- 1/4 cup of crumbled feta cheese (optional)
- 2 whole-wheat pita breads, toasted (optional)

Instructions

1. Prepare the steamer: Follow the directions that came with your electric steamer to add water. Warm up the steamer while you get the food ready.
2. Saute vegetables: Set olive oil on medium heat in a large pan or skillet. You should cook the onion and bell pepper for 5 minutes or until they get soft. Add the garlic, stir it in, and cook for one more minute until it smells good.
3. Season and crumble chickpeas: Spice it with salt, pepper, chili powder, turmeric, and cumin. Mix everything, then cook for 30 seconds. For a "scrambled" texture, use a fork to break up half of the chickpeas
4. Steam vegetables: The chickpeas and vegetables should be put in the steamer basket. You can add cherry tomatoes on top if you want to—steam for 15 to 20 minutes or until the chickpeas are hot and the vegetables are soft.
5. Assemble and serve: Split the steamed mix between two bowls. If you want to, add toasted pita bread, crumbled feta cheese, and fresh cilantro. Have fun, hot!

3. RAINBOW VEGGIE FRITTATA STACKS

Prep Time: 15 minutes | Cook Time: 25 minutes

Total Time: 40 minutes | Serving: 2

Ingredients

- 1/4 tsp black pepper
- 1/4 tsp dried oregano
- 1/4 cup of chopped fresh spinach
- 1/4 tsp salt
- 1/4 cup of unsweetened plant-based milk
- 1/2 cup of chopped orange bell pepper
- 1/4 cup of chopped cherry tomatoes
- 1/2 cup of chopped green bell pepper
- 1/2 cup of chopped red bell pepper
- 1 tbsp olive oil
- 1/2 cup of chopped zucchini
- 4 large eggs
- 1/4 cup of grated Parmesan cheese (optional)

Instructions

1. Prepare the steamer: Follow the manufacturer's instructions to fill your electric steamer with water and heat it.
2. Whisk batter: Add the eggs, milk, oregano, salt, pepper, and Parmesan cheese (if using) to a large bowl. Use a whisk to mix the ingredients well.
3. Saute vegetables: Warm up a big pan with olive oil over medium-low heat. After you add the zucchini and bell peppers, cook for 5 minutes or until the vegetables get soft. Put the cherry tomatoes in and stir them in. Cook for one more minute.
4. Assemble in steamer: Grease two ramekins or small bowls that can go in the oven. Spread the vegetables that have been sauteed out evenly in the ramekins. Cover the vegetables with the egg mixture, ensuring each ramekin is almost complete.
5. Steam and cook: Be careful when putting the ramekins in the steamer basket—steam for 15 to 20 minutes or until the frittatas are set and cooked through. To check if it's done, stick a toothpick into the middle and pull it out clean.
6. Assemble and serve: Before flipping the frittatas over onto plates, let them cool a bit. Put fresh spinach on top and eat it hot.

4. HONEY-MUSTARD GLAZED SALMON

Prep Time: 10 minutes | Cook Time: 20 minutes

Total Time: 30 minutes | Serving: 2

Ingredients

For the salmon:

- 1 tbsp Dijon mustard
- 1 tbsp honey
- 2 (6 ounce) salmon fillets, skin on or off (your preference)
- 1/2 tsp dried thyme
- 1 tbsp olive oil
- Salt and pepper to taste

For the steamed veggies:

- 1 cup of baby carrots, halved
- 1/2 cup of cherry tomatoes
- 1 cup of broccoli florets
- 1/4 cup of chopped fresh parsley (optional)

Instructions

1. Prepare the steamer: Fill your electric steamer with water according to the manufacturer's instructions and preheat.
2. Make the glaze: In a small bowl, whisk together the Dijon mustard, honey, olive oil, and thyme. Season with salt and pepper to taste.
3. Prepare the salmon: Pat the salmon fillets dry with paper towels. Brush each fillet with the honey-mustard glaze, ensuring all sides are coated.
4. Steam the veggies: Place the broccoli florets, carrots, and cherry tomatoes in the steamer basket.
5. Steam the salmon: Place the salmon fillets on a steam tray or rack (not directly on the vegetables) above the veggie basket.
6. Steam together: Steam for 15-20 minutes, or until the salmon is cooked through (internal temperature reaches 145°F) and the vegetables are tender-crisp.
7. Serve: Divide the steamed vegetables between two plates. Top each with a glazed salmon fillet. Garnish with fresh parsley (optional) and enjoy!

5. RAINBOW DUMPLING DELIGHT

Prep Time: 20 minutes | Cook Time: 15 minutes

Total Time: 35 minutes | Serving: 4

Ingredients

For the dumpling wrappers:

- 1 ½ cups of all-purpose flour
- ½ cup of warm water
- Food coloring (red, orange, yellow, green, purple)

For the filling:

- ¼ cup of chopped fresh cilantro
- ½ tsp sesame oil
- ½ cup of shredded carrots
- 1 tbsp soy sauce
- ½ cup of chopped mushrooms
- ½ cup of shredded red cabbage
- ½ cup of diced green bell pepper
- ¼ tsp ground ginger
- 2 cloves garlic, minced
- Salt and pepper to taste

For dipping sauce:

- 1 tbsp rice vinegar
- 1 tsp sesame oil
- 1 tbsp soy sauce
- 1 tsp sriracha sauce (optional, for spice)
- Chopped scallions (for garnish)

Instructions

1. Gather the flour and divide it into five equal bowls. Use these to make the dumpling wrappers. Put a few drops of food coloring into each bowl to make red, yellow, orange, green, and purple dough. Add warm water to each bowl until a soft dough forms. For 5 minutes, knead each dough until it is smooth and springy. Wrap it up in plastic wrap and set it aside for 10 minutes.
2. Prepare the filling: Mix all the filling items in a large bowl. After mixing well, set it aside.
3. To put the dumplings together, roll out a thin circle of each color of dough on a lightly floured surface. Cut each piece of dough into a 3-inch circle with a cookie cutter.
4. Put some filling in the middle of each circle of dough. To make a crescent shape, wet the edges of the circle and fold it in half. To make a tight seal, pinch the edges. Do it again with the rest of the dough and filling.
5. To steam the dumplings, follow the directions on the package and fill your electric steamer with water. Then, bring it to a boil. Use parchment paper or a silicone steamer mat to line the steamer basket. Ensure the dumplings don't touch each other as you put them in the basket.
6. Place the dumplings in a steamer and cover it. Steam them for 15 minutes or until the filling is cooked through and the dumplings are clear.
7. Make the dipping sauce. Put all the ingredients for the dipping sauce in a small bowl and whisk them together while the dumplings are steaming.
8. Put out: Put the steamed dumplings on a plate and give the sauce to go with them. Add chopped scallions as a garnish if you want to.

6. STEAMED OATMEAL WITH BERRIES AND CHIA SEEDS

Prep Time: 5 minutes | Cook Time: 15 minutes

Total Time: 20 minutes | Serving: 1

Ingredients

- 1 cup of Water or milk
- 1/4 cup of Fresh or frozen berries
- 1/2 cup of Rolled oats
- Pinch of salt
- 1 tbsp Chia seeds
- Optional toppings: honey, maple syrup, chopped nuts, sliced banana, shredded coconut flakes

Instructions

1. Put the oats, water or milk, and salt in the basket of your electric steamer.
2. Pick your favorite berries and add them.
3. Add chia seeds on top.
4. Follow the cooking time directions that came with your steamer. For rolled oats, aim for 15 minutes. If you want quick oats or more steamer power, change the time.
5. Prepare your toppings (if you want) while the oatmeal cooks.
6. Use a fork to fluff the oatmeal after it's done cooking.
7. Put oatmeal into a bowl and add any toppings you like on top of it. Enjoy!

7. ASIAN-STYLE STEAMED BUNS WITH EGGS

Prep Time: 30 minutes | Cook Time: 15 minutes

Total Time: 45 minutes | Serving: 6-8 buns

Ingredients

For the dough:

- 1 tbsp sugar
- 1 tbsp vegetable oil
- 1 tsp instant yeast
- 1/3 cup of warm water (105°F)
- 1/3 cup of milk (warm)
- 1/2 tsp salt
- 2 cups of all-purpose flour

For the filling:

- 1 tbsp oyster sauce
- 1 tsp sesame oil
- 1/4 tsp black pepper
- 1 tbsp soy sauce
- 4 eggs, hard-boiled and peeled
- 1/4 cup of chopped scallions
- Optional: Chopped cooked chicken or pork, shredded vegetables

Instructions

Prepare the dough:

1. Mix the sugar, flour, yeast, and salt in a big bowl. Mix it up nicely.
2. Mix warm water, milk, and vegetable oil in a different bowl using a whisk.
3. Combine the wet and dry ingredients slowly while mixing them together until a shaggy dough forms.
4. The dough should be kneaded on a lightly floured surface for eight to ten minutes or until it is smooth and elastic.
5. Put the dough in a bowl with greased plastic wrap. It should rise in a warm place for an hour or until it gets twice as big.

Prepare the filling:

1. Use a fork to break up the hard-boiled eggs into big chunks.
2. Add scallions, soy sauce, oyster sauce, sesame oil, and black pepper to the mashed eggs. Combine well.
3. You can add cooked chicken, pork, or shredded vegetables to the filling for more flavor and protein.

Assemble and steam the buns:

1. The dough has risen, so punch it down and cut it into 6 to 8 equal pieces.
2. Form a ball out of each piece and then press it down into a small disc.
3. Put a small amount of filling in the middle of each disc.
4. To make a bun, pinch the edges of the dough together around the filling.
5. Use parchment paper or a silicone steamer mat to line the basket of your electric steamer.
6. Make sure the buns have room to rise by putting them in the basket.
7. Follow the directions on the package to fill your steamer with water and then bring it to a boil.
8. Put the basket of the steamer over the pot of boiling water. Steam for 15 minutes, or until the buns are fully cooked and slightly see-through.

Serve:

1. Take the buns out of the steamer and let them cool down before serving them.
2. Dip the buns in your favorite sauce, like soy sauce, chili oil, or hoisin sauce, while they are still warm.

8. SAVORY SALMON STEAM BUNS

Prep Time: 20 minutes | Cook Time: 15 minutes

Total Time: 35 minutes | Serving: 4-6 buns

Ingredients

For the dough:

- 1 1/2 cups of all-purpose flour
- 1/3 cup of warm water (105°F)
- 1 tsp instant yeast
- 1/4 tsp salt
- 1/3 cup of milk (warm)
- 1/2 tsp sugar
- 1 tbsp vegetable oil

For the filling:

- 1 tsp Sriracha sauce (optional, for spice)
- 8 ounce skinless, boneless salmon fillet, cooked and flaked
- 1/4 cup of chopped green onions
- 1/4 tsp garlic powder
- 2 tbsp soy sauce
- 1 tbsp sesame oil
- 1/2 tsp grated ginger
- Pinch of black pepper

For steaming:

- Parchment paper or silicone steamer mat

Instructions

Make the dough:

1. Combine the sugar, yeast, salt, and flour in a big bowl with a whisk.
2. Mix the warm water, milk, and vegetable oil in a different bowl.
3. Slowly put the wet ingredients into the dry ones and mix them together until a shaggy dough forms.
4. Place the dough on a lightly floured surface and work it into a smooth, elastic ball for 8 to 10 minutes.
5. Over a greased bowl, put the dough. Cover with plastic wrap. Set the bowl somewhere warm for an hour or until the dough grows double in size.

Prepare the filling:

1. As the dough rises, cook the salmon however you like (grilling, baking, or poaching) until it is fully cooked. Flake the cooked salmon with a fork.
2. Flaked salmon, green onions, soy sauce, sesame oil, Sriracha (if using), ginger, garlic powder, and black pepper should all be put in a bowl together. Combine well.

Assemble and steam the buns:

1. After the dough has risen, punch it down and cut it into 4 to 6 equal pieces.
2. Form a ball from each piece and press it into a small disc.
3. Put a small amount of filling in the middle of each disc.
4. To make a bun, pinch the edges of the dough together around the filling.
5. Use parchment paper or a silicone steamer mat to line the basket of your electric steamer.
6. Place the buns in the basket so they have room to rise.
7. Follow the directions on the package to fill your steamer with water and then bring it to a boil.
8. Put the steamer basket over the pot of boiling water—steam for 15 minutes or until the buns are fully cooked and slightly see-through.

Serve:

1. Take the buns out of the steamer and let them cool down a bit before you serve them.
2. Dip the buns in your favorite sauce, like soy sauce, chili oil, or hoisin sauce, while they are still warm.

9. SPINACH AND FETA FRITTATA CUPS

Prep Time: 15 minutes | Cook Time: 20 minutes

Total Time: 35 minutes | Serving: 4

Ingredients

- 4 large eggs
- 1/4 tsp dried oregano
- 1/4 cup of crumbled feta cheese
- 1/4 cup of chopped fresh spinach
- 1/4 cup of diced cherry tomatoes
- 1 tbsp olive oil
- 1/4 cup of chopped red onion
- 1/4 cup of milk (any kind)
- Salt and pepper to taste
- Optional: Chopped fresh parsley for garnish

Instructions

1. Get the steamer ready: Follow the manufacturer's instructions to fill your electric steamer with water and heat it. Grease four ramekins or small bowls that can go in the oven.
2. Beat the eggs. Put the eggs, milk, feta cheese, oregano, salt, and pepper in a large bowl and beat them with a whisk until they are well mixed.
3. I put olive oil in a pan and heated it over medium-low heat. After you add the onion, cook for about two minutes until it gets soft. Add the spinach and tomatoes and stir them in. Cook for about one minute until the spinach wilts.
4. Put the cups of together: Put the sauteed vegetables in each of the ramekins that have been prepared. Fill almost all the ramekins with the egg mixture before pouring it over the vegetables.
5. Put the ramekins with the frittatas in a steamer basket—steam for 15 to 20 minutes or until the frittatas are set and cooked through. Simply insert a toothpick into the middle and remove it cleanly to see if it's done.
6. Serve: Turn the frittatas over onto plates after letting them cool a bit. Add fresh parsley if you want, and serve warm.

10. STEAMED ASPARAGUS AND POACHED EGG CROISSANTS

Prep Time: 15 minutes | Cook Time: 15 minutes

Total Time: 30 minutes | Serving: 2

Ingredients

- 2 large croissants, split in half horizontally
- 1/4 cup of water
- 2 large eggs
- 4 spears fresh asparagus, trimmed
- 1 tbsp white vinegar
- Salt and pepper to taste
- Optional toppings: Chopped chives, hollandaise sauce, hot sauce

Instructions

1. Get the steamer ready: Follow the manufacturer's instructions to fill your electric steamer with water and heat it.
2. Warm up the croissants: Warm the croissant halves up in a toaster or under the broiler until they turn golden brown.
3. To steam the asparagus, put it in the steamer basket and steam it for 5 minutes or until it is soft but still crisp.
4. First, bring a large pot of water to a simmer. Then, add the eggs and poach them. To make a vortex, add the vinegar and stir it in. Put a cracked egg in a small bowl. Put the eggs slowly into the water that is simmering. As soon as the whites start to set, add the yolks and cook for another three to four minutes.
5. Please take a look: Toast one half of a croissant and put it on each plate. Add spears of steamed asparagus on top. Put one poached egg on top of each pile of asparagus. Carefully remove the eggs from the water with a slotted spoon.
6. Add pepper and salt to taste.
7. Serve: Drizzle with your favorite toppings (not required) and eat immediately!

11. STEAMED BREAKFAST BURRITO BOWLS

Prep Time: 15 minutes | Cook Time: 15 minutes

Total Time: 30 minutes | Serving: 2

Ingredients

For the filling:

- 1 cup of chopped sweet potato
- 1/4 cup of chopped fresh cilantro
- 1/2 tsp chili powder
- 1/4 tsp cumin
- 1/4 cup of corn kernels
- 1 tbsp olive oil
- 1/2 cup of chopped bell pepper
- 1/2 cup of chopped onion
- 1/4 cup of black beans, rinsed and drained
- Pinch of salt and pepper

For the protein (choose one or two):

- 1/4 cup of crumbled tofu
- 1 cooked and crumbled breakfast sausage patty
- 2 scrambled eggs
- 1/2 cup of cooked and shredded chicken breast

Other toppings (optional):

- Sour cream
- Diced tomato
- Hot sauce
- Salsa
- Whole wheat tortillas, warmed (for wrapping)
- Sliced avocado
- Shredded cheese

Instructions

1. Get the steamer ready: Follow the manufacturer's instructions to fill your electric steamer with water and heat it up.
2. Mix the ingredients for the filling: Cut up the sweet potato and put it in a large bowl. Put the onion, bell pepper, black beans, corn, cilantro, cumin, salt, and pepper. Toss everything to cover it all.
3. Heat the filling up: Put the vegetables in the steamer basket and steam for 10 to 12 minutes, or until the vegetables are fully cooked and the sweet potato is soft.
4. Prepare your meat: While the vegetables are steaming, make your protein of choice in any way you like (scrambled eggs, pan-fried sausage, shredded chicken, etc.).
5. Put the bowls together: Put some of the steamed vegetables into each of two bowls. Add the protein of your choice and any toppings you like, like salsa, avocado, tomato, cheese, etc.
6. Serve: You can eat it warm in a bowl or wrap it in a whole wheat tortilla (optional).

12. POACHED EGGS FLORENTINE

Prep Time: 15 minutes | Cook Time: 20 minutes

Total Time: 35 minutes | Serving: 2

Ingredients

- 1/4 cup of Hollandaise sauce
- 1 cup of baby spinach, washed and dried
- 1 tbsp white vinegar
- 2 English muffins, split and toasted
- 2 large eggs
- Salt and pepper to taste

Optional garnish:

- Chopped fresh chives
- Sliced cherry tomatoes

Instructions

1. Get the steamer ready: Follow the directions on the package to fill your electric steamer with water and then bring it to a simmer.
2. Warm up the English muffins: Toast both halves of the English muffin until they turn golden brown.
3. To make the spinach, put it in a bowl that can be put in the microwave and heated for 30 seconds until it wilts. You could also use the steamer basket to wilt the spinach in 3–4 minutes.
4. Poach the eggs by adding vinegar to water that is already very hot. Make a swirl in the water with a spoon. Break each egg into a tiny bowl, then carefully put them into the swirling water. As soon as the whites start to set, add the yolks and cook for another three to four minutes.
5. Take a look: Put half of the toasted English muffins on two plates. Put some wilted spinach on top of each one.
6. Take out the poached eggs. Carefully remove the eggs from the water with a slotted spoon and place them on top of the spinach.
7. Add sauce: Put the Hollandaise sauce on top of the eggs and spinach.
8. Make it taste good: Add salt and pepper to taste. You can add chopped chives and sliced cherry tomatoes as a garnish.

SNACKS AND APPETIZERS

13. STEAMED SHRIMP AND ASPARAGUS PARCELS

Prep Time: 15 minutes | Cook Time: 12 minutes

Total Time: 27 minutes | Serving: 2

Ingredients

- 4 large squares parchment paper
- 1 tbsp lemon juice
- 1/4 tsp garlic powder
- 4 large asparagus spears, trimmed and tough ends removed
- 1/2 tsp dried dill
- 8 large shrimp, peeled and deveined
- 1 tbsp olive oil
- Salt and pepper to taste
- Optional garnish: Chopped fresh parsley

Instructions

1. Get the steamer ready: Follow the directions on the package to fill your electric steamer with water and then bring it to a boil.
2. Get the filling ready: Salt, pepper, lemon juice, dill, and olive oil should all be put in a bowl. Toss the shrimp around in the mixture to cover them all.
3. Put the packages together: Put a square of parchment paper on a flat surface. Along the middle line, put two spears of asparagus next to each other. Leave some space around the edges. Put two shrimp on top of the asparagus. Be careful as you fold the sides of the parchment paper over the filling. Then, fold the top and bottom down to seal the envelope. Do it again with the rest of the ingredients and parchment paper.
4. Put the packages in steam: Place the packages in the steamer basket so that they don't touch each other. For 12 minutes, or until the shrimp are opaque and cooked all the way through, steam them.
5. Serve: Carefully open the packages and put the food on plates. Add any pan juices that are still left over, and, if you want, sprinkle chopped parsley on top.

14. SPICY STEAMED MUSSELS

Prep Time: 10 minutes | Cook Time: 10 minutes

Total Time: 20 minutes | Serving: 2-3

Ingredients

- 1 tbsp chopped garlic
- 1 tsp lemon juice
- 1/2 cup of white wine or vegetable broth
- 1 tbsp chopped fresh cilantro
- 1 tbsp olive oil
- 1 tbsp chopped ginger
- 1/2 tsp turmeric powder
- 1/4 tsp smoked paprika
- 1/4 tsp cumin
- 2 pounds mussels, debearded and cleaned
- 1/2 red chili pepper, finely chopped (adjust for desired spice level)
- Salt and pepper to taste

Instructions

1. Get the steamer ready: Follow the directions on the package to fill your electric steamer with water and then bring it to a boil.
2. Clean and throw away any mussels that are broken or open. Run cold water over the mussels after you're done cleaning them.
3. Put the olive oil in a big pan and heat it over medium-low heat. Put in the chili pepper, garlic, and ginger. Cook for 30 seconds, until the food smells good.
4. Use white wine or broth to clean out the pan. You can add the cumin, turmeric, paprika, and lemon juice after cutting the cilantro up. Add pepper and salt.
5. Move the mussel mix to the basket of the steamer. Place the mussels on top, making sure they don't touch.
6. They should be steamed for 5 to 7 minutes, or until they open up and are fully cooked. Don't eat any mussels that aren't open.
7. Serve right away. Move the mussels to a serving platter or individual bowls using tongs. Pour the tasty cooking liquid over the mussels. Put it out with some crusty bread for dipping.

15. VEGETABLE SHUMAI

Prep Time: 15 minutes | Cook Time: 12 minutes

Total Time: 27 minutes | Serving: 4

Ingredients

For the filling:

- 1/4 cup of chopped green onions
- 1 cup of shredded cabbage (napa or green cabbage)
- 2 tbsp soy sauce
- 1/2 cup of chopped mushrooms
- 1 tbsp rice vinegar
- 1 tbsp sesame oil
- 1/2 tsp garlic powder
- 1 tsp grated ginger
- 1 cup of diced carrots
- Salt and pepper to taste

For the wrappers:

- 24 wonton wrappers

For steaming:

- Parchment paper or silicone steamer mat

Instructions

1. Get the steamer ready: Follow the directions on the package to fill your electric steamer with water and then bring it to a boil. Use parchment paper or a silicone steamer mat to line the steamer basket.
2. Fill the shell: Shred the cabbage, dice the carrots, chop the mushrooms, and mix the green onions and mushrooms in a large bowl.
3. Season the filling with: Put the vegetables in a bowl and season them with salt, rice vinegar, ginger, pepper, soy sauce, and sesame oil. Make sure all the ingredients are coated evenly by mixing them together well.
4. Put together the shumai: A wonton wrapper should be laid out on a flat surface. Leave some space around the edges and put a tbsp of filling in the middle. Bring the wrapper's corners together in the middle and pinch them together to make a pouch. Do it again with the rest of the wrappers and filling.
5. To steam the shumai, put the assembled shumai in the steamer basket that has been prepared, making sure they don't touch. Put them in the steamer for 12 minutes, or until the filling is done and the wrappers are clear.
6. To serve, carefully take the shumai out of the steamer and put them on plates. You can serve it hot with soy sauce, chili oil, hoisin sauce, or any other sauce you like.

16. VEGETABLE AND CORN DUMPLINGS

Prep Time: 20 minutes | Cook Time: 15 minutes

Total Time: 35 minutes | Serving: 4

Ingredients

For the dumpling wrappers:
- ½ cup of lukewarm water
- 1 ½ cups of all-purpose flour
- Pinch of salt

For the filling:

- 2 tbsp soy sauce
- 1 tsp sesame oil
- ½ cup of diced carrots
- 1/4 cup of chopped green onions
- 1 ½ cups of shredded cabbage
- 1/2 tsp grated ginger
- 1 cup of frozen corn kernels, thawed
- 1 tbsp oyster sauce (optional)
- Salt and pepper to taste

For steaming:

- Parchment paper or silicone steamer mat

Instructions

Prepare the dumpling wrappers:

1. Combine the flour and salt in a huge bowl. Slowly add lukewarm water while mixing until a shaggy dough forms.
2. Lay out some flour on a surface. Knead the dough for five to seven minutes, or until it is smooth and springy. Put a damp cloth over it and let it rest for 10 minutes.

Prepare the filling:

1. Shred the cabbage and put it in a bowl. Add the corn kernels, carrots, and green onions.
2. Add soy sauce, oyster sauce (if you want), sesame oil, ginger, salt, and pepper to the vegetables. Make sure all the ingredients are coated evenly by mixing them together well.

Assemble and steam the dumplings:

1. Split the dough into 24 equal pieces. Use a rolling pin to make a thin circle out of each piece.
2. Put some filling in the middle of each circle of dough.
3. To make a crescent shape or your favorite dumpling fold, pinch the edges of the dough together to cover the filling.
4. Follow the directions on the package to fill your electric steamer with water and then bring it to a boil. Use parchment paper or a silicone steamer mat to line the steamer basket.
5. Ensure the dumplings don't touch each other as you put them in the basket.
6. Put them in the steamer for 15 minutes or until the filling and wrappers are transparent.

Serve:

1. Carefully take the dumplings out of the steamer and put them on plates.
2. You can serve it hot with soy sauce, chili oil, hoisin sauce, or any other sauce you like.

17. VEGETABLE GYOZA POTSTICKERS

Prep Time: 20 minutes | Cook Time: 15 minutes

Total Time: 35 minutes | Serving: 4

Ingredients

For the dumpling wrappers:

- 1 ½ cups of all-purpose flour
- ½ cup of lukewarm water
- Pinch of salt

For the filling:

- ½ cup of chopped green onions
- ¼ cup of diced carrots
- 1 ½ cups of shredded napa cabbage
- 1 cup of chopped mushrooms (shiitake or mixed)
- 1 tbsp sesame oil
- 1 tsp grated ginger
- ½ tsp garlic powder
- 2 tbsp soy sauce
- Salt and pepper to taste

For steaming and frying:

- Vegetable oil
- Parchment paper or silicone steamer mat

Instructions

Prepare the dumpling wrappers:

1. Mix the flour and salt in a huge bowl. Add lukewarm water slowly while mixing until a shaggy dough forms.
2. To make the dough smooth and stretchy, knead it on a lightly floured surface for five to seven minutes. Ten minutes of rest after covering with a damp cloth.

Prepare the filling:

1. Shred the cabbage and put it in a bowl. Add the mushrooms, green onions, and carrots.
2. Spice up the vegetables with soy sauce, sesame oil, ginger, garlic powder, salt, and pepper. Make sure all the ingredients are coated evenly by mixing them together well.

Assemble and steam the gyoza:

1. Split the dough into 24 equal pieces. Use a rolling pin to make a thin circle out of each piece.
2. Put some filling in the middle of each circle of dough.
3. To make a traditional gyoza fold, pinch the edges of the dough together to make a crescent shape with wrinkles around the filling.
4. Follow the directions on the package to fill your electric steamer with water and then bring it to a boil. Use parchment paper or a silicone steamer mat to line the steamer basket.
5. Make sure the gyoza don't touch each other as you put them in the basket.
6. Put them in the steamer for 10 minutes or until the filling and wrappers are clear.

Fry the potstickers (optional):

1. Put a small amount of oil in a big pan and heat it over medium-low heat.
2. Move the steamed gyoza carefully to the pan, leaving some space between them.
3. On each side, it takes about two to three minutes until the bottoms are golden brown and crispy.
4. Add a little water to the pan and close the lid tightly for one minute to make it taste like it was steamed and then fried.

Serve:

1. Serve the gyoza hot with your favorite dipping sauce, like chili oil, soy sauce, or a mix of soy sauce, rice vinegar, and sesame oil.

18. STEAMED EDAMAME AND TOFU SPRING ROLLS

Prep Time: 20 minutes | Cook Time: 15 minutes | Total Time: 35 minutes | Serving: 4

Ingredients

For the spring rolls:

- 1/4 cup of chopped cucumber
- 1 block (14 ounce) firm tofu, drained and patted dry
- 1/2 cup of shredded carrots
- 1 cup of cooked and shelled edamame
- 1 tsp sesame oil
- 1/4 cup of chopped fresh cilantro
- 12 rice paper wrappers
- 1/4 cup of chopped green onions
- 1 tbsp rice vinegar
- 1 tbsp soy sauce
- Salt and pepper to taste

For steaming:

- Parchment paper or silicone steamer mat

Instructions

Prepare the filling:

1. Break up the tofu and put it in a bowl. Mix the cooked edamame with the chopped cucumber, green onions, cilantro, and shredded carrots in a bowl.
2. Mix soy sauce, rice vinegar, sesame oil, salt, and pepper in a different bowl using a whisk. Add the dressing to the tofu and vegetable mix and mix it all together.

Assemble and steam the spring rolls:

1. Put warm water in a big bowl. A 15-second soak in water should make one rice paper wrapper soft but not wet.
2. Place the warmed wrapper flat on a plate. Put some of the fillings close to the bottom edge of the wrapper.
3. Put the filling inside the wrapper and fold the bottom edge over it. Next, tuck the sides of the wrapper very close together. Roll the wrapper up so that it completely covers the filling. Please do it again with the rest of the wrappers and filling.
4. Follow the directions on the package to fill your electric steamer with water and then bring it to a boil. Use parchment paper or a silicone steamer mat to line the steamer basket. Place the spring rolls in the basket so they don't touch each other.
5. Steam the food for 10 to 12 minutes, or until the filling is hot all the way through and the rice paper wrappers clear up.
6. Carefully take the spring rolls out of the steamer and put them on a plate.
7. If you want to dip it in something, you can use soy sauce, chili oil, or peanut sauce. Serve it hot.

19. STEAMED CHICKEN & BROCCOLI BUNS

Prep Time: 20 minutes | Cook Time: 15 minutes

Total Time: 35 minutes | Serving: 4-6 buns

Ingredients

For the dough:

- 1/2 tsp sugar
- 1/3 cup of milk (warm)
- 1 tsp instant yeast
- 1 1/2 cups of all-purpose flour
- 1/4 tsp salt
- 1/3 cup of warm water (105°F)
- 1 tbsp vegetable oil

For the filling:

- 8 ounce skinless, boneless chicken breast, cooked and shredded
- 2 tbsp soy sauce
- 1/4 cup of chopped green onions
- 1/2 cup of chopped broccoli florets
- 1 tsp grated ginger
- 1 tbsp sesame oil
- 1/2 tsp garlic powder
- Pinch of black pepper

For steaming:

- Parchment paper or silicone steamer mat

Instructions

Make the dough:

1. Mix the yeast, salt, sugar, and flour in a large bowl with a whisk.
2. Mix the warm water, milk, and vegetable oil in a different bowl.
3. Slowly put the wet ingredients into the dry ones and mix them together until a shaggy dough forms.
4. Place the dough on a lightly floured surface and work it into a smooth, elastic ball for 8 to 10 minutes.
5. Over a greased bowl, put the dough. Cover with plastic wrap. Putting the bowl somewhere warm will make the dough double in size in an hour.

Prepare the filling:

1. As the dough rises, cook the chicken breast however you like (grilling, baking, poaching) until it is fully cooked. Shred the cooked chicken with two forks.
2. In an electric steamer, cook the broccoli florets for 5 to 7 minutes until they are soft but still crisp. Let it cool down a bit, then cut it up into little pieces.
3. Shred the chicken and put it in a bowl. Add the broccoli, green onions, soy sauce, sesame oil, ginger, garlic powder, and black pepper. Combine well by mixing.

Assemble and steam the buns:

1. After the dough has risen, punch it down and cut it into 4 to 6 equal pieces.
2. Form a ball out of each piece and then press it down into a small disc.
3. Put a small amount of filling in the middle of each disc.
4. To make a bun, pinch the edges of the dough together around the filling.
5. Follow the directions on the package to fill your electric steamer with water and then bring it to a boil. Use parchment paper or a silicone steamer mat to line the steamer basket.
6. Place the buns in the basket so that they have some room to rise.
7. The buns should be steamed for 15 minutes, or until they are fully cooked and a little see-through.

Serve:

1. Take the buns out of the steamer and let them cool down before serving them.
2. Dip the buns in your favorite sauce, like soy sauce, chili oil, or hoisin sauce, while they are still warm.

20. STEAMED CHICKEN POTSTICKERS

Prep Time: 20 minutes | Cook Time: 15 minutes

Total Time: 35 minutes | Serving: 4

Ingredients

For the filling:

- 1/2 tsp garlic powder
- 1/2 cup of shredded cabbage (napa or green cabbage)
- 1 tsp grated ginger
- 1 pound ground chicken
- 2 tbsp soy sauce
- 1/4 cup of chopped green onions
- 1 tbsp sesame oil
- 1 tbsp oyster sauce (optional)
- Salt and pepper to taste

For the wrappers and steaming:

- Parchment paper or silicone steamer mat
- Vegetable oil (optional, for pan-frying)
- 24 wonton wrappers

Instructions

Prepare the filling:

1. Put shredded cabbage, green onions, soy sauce, oyster sauce (if you want), sesame oil, ginger, garlic powder, salt, and pepper in a huge bowl. Make sure all the ingredients are spread out evenly by mixing them well.

Assemble the potstickers:

2. A wonton wrapper should be laid out on a flat surface. Leave some space around the edges and put a tbsp of filling in the middle.
3. Use water to wet the edges of the wrapper. To make a half-moon shape, fold one side of the wrapper over the filling. To seal, pinch the edges together and make folds or pleats along the seam. Do it again with the rest of the wrappers and filling.

Steam the potstickers:

1. Follow the directions on the package to fill your electric steamer with water and then bring it to a boil. Use parchment paper or a silicone steamer mat to line the steamer basket.
2. Place the potstickers in the basket so they don't touch each other.
3. Steam for 12 to 15 minutes or until the wrappers are clear and the filling is cooked all the way through.

Optional pan-frying:

1. Put a small amount of oil in a big pan and heat it over medium-low heat.
2. Move the steamed potstickers carefully to the pan, leaving some space between them.
3. It should be cooked on each side for two to three minutes until it turns golden brown and crispy.

Serve:

1. Place the potstickers on a plate and serve them hot with soy sauce, chili oil, or hoisin sauce, or any other sauce you like.

21. STEAMED CHICKEN AND MUSHROOM SHU MAI

Prep Time: 15 minutes | Cook Time: 12 minutes

Total Time: 27 minutes | Serving: 4

Ingredients

For the filling:

- 1 tbsp sesame oil
- 1 tbsp rice vinegar
- 1/4 cup of chopped green onions
- 1/2 pound ground chicken
- 1 tsp grated ginger
- 1/2 tsp garlic powder
- 2 tbsp soy sauce
- 1/2 cup of finely chopped shiitake mushrooms
- Pinch of white pepper
- Salt to taste

For the wrappers and steaming:

- 24 wonton wrappers
- Parchment paper or silicone steamer mat

Instructions

1. Get the filling ready. Put chopped mushrooms, green onions, soy sauce, rice vinegar, sesame oil, ginger, garlic powder, white pepper, salt, and white pepper into a large bowl. Please make sure all the ingredients are spread out evenly by mixing them well.
2. In order to put the shumai together, lay a wonton wrapper out on a flat surface. Leave some space around the edges and put a tbsp of filling in the middle.
3. Bring the wrapper's corners in the middle and pinch them together to make a pouch. You can also make pleats around the sides for a traditional shumai look.
4. Do it again with the rest of the wrappers and filling.
5. Follow the manufacturer's instructions for the shumai and fill your electric steamer with water. Then, bring it to a boil. Use parchment paper or a silicone steamer mat to line the steamer basket.
6. Place the shumai that has been put together so they don't touch the basket.
7. Steam for 12 to 15 minutes or until the wrappers are clear and the filling is cooked.
8. To serve, carefully take the shumai from the steamer and put it on a plate.
9. You can serve it hot with soy sauce, chili oil, hoisin sauce, or any other sauce you like.

22. STEAMED FISH BAO

Prep Time: 20 minutes | Cook Time: 15 minutes

Total Time: 35 minutes | Serving: 4

Ingredients

For the bao buns:

- 1/3 cup of lukewarm milk
- ½ tsp salt
- 1 ¾ tsp active dry yeast
- 1 tbsp sugar
- 1 tbsp vegetable oil
- 1/3 cup of warm water
- 1 ½ cups of all-purpose flour

For the fish filling:

- 1/2 tsp grated ginger
- 1 tsp sesame oil
- 1/4 tsp garlic powder
- 12 ounce white fish fillets, skinless and boneless
- 1 tbsp rice vinegar
- 2 tbsp soy sauce
- 1 tbsp oyster sauce (optional)
- Pinch of white pepper
- Scallions, thinly sliced (for garnish)

For steaming:

- Parchment paper or silicone steamer mat

Instructions:

1. To make the bao buns, mix the yeast, flour, salt, and sugar in a huge bowl.
2. Mix the warm milk, water, and oil in a different bowl.
3. Slowly add the wet items to the dry ones and mix them together until a shaggy dough forms.
4. Place the dough on a lightly floured surface and work it into a smooth, elastic ball for 8 to 10 minutes.
5. Over a greased bowl, put the dough. Cover with plastic wrap. Putting the bowl somewhere warm will make the dough double in size in an hour.
6. As the dough rises, cut the fish fillets into small pieces that are ready to be put inside.
7. Put soy sauce, rice vinegar, ginger, garlic powder, white pepper, oyster sauce (if you want), sesame oil, and oyster sauce in a bowl.
8. Put the fish pieces in the sauce and sit for 10 minutes.
9. Put the bao together and steam it. Punch down the dough that has risen and cut it into 12 equal pieces.
10. Form a ball out of each piece and press it down into a small disc.
11. Fill the middle of each disc with a spoonful of fish that has been marinated.
12. Bring the dough's edges in the middle and pinch them together to seal the filling inside. Leave a small opening at the top.

13. Follow the directions on the package to fill your electric steamer with water and then bring it to a boil. Use parchment paper or a silicone steamer mat to line the steamer basket.
14. Place the bao in the basket, ensuring they have little room to rise.
15. The buns should be steamed for 15 minutes until fully cooked and a little see-through.
16. To serve, carefully take the bao out of the steamer and put it on a plate.
17. Add thinly sliced scallions as a garnish and serve hot.

23. STEAMED EDAMAME PODS

Prep Time: 5 minutes | Cook Time: 5-7 minutes

Total Time: 10-12 minutes | Serving: 2-3

Ingredients

- 1 pound frozen edamame pods (shelled or in the pod)
- 1/2 tbsp olive oil (optional)
- 1/2 tsp sea salt (optional)
- Pinch of crushed red pepper flakes (optional)

Instructions

Getting the steamer ready:

1. Follow the directions on the package to fill your electric steamer with water and then bring it to a boil.
2. Getting the edamame ready: Rinse the edamame pods under cold running water if you want to use them in their shells. To get the beans out, pinch the seam of each pod with your thumbs and pull. Throw away the pods.
3. Run cold water over the shelled edamame to clean them.
4. Seasoning (optional): Put the edamame in a bowl and add any seasonings you want, like red pepper flakes, sea salt, or olive oil. Add toss to cover evenly.
5. For steaming, put the edamame, either seasoned or not, in the steamer basket.
6. Steam it for 5 to 7 minutes or until the edamame is hot all the way through and just slightly crunchy. You can taste a few to see if they're right.
7. To serve, carefully take the edamame out of the steamer and put it in a bowl.
8. Serve the edamame right away and enjoy it hot or warm.

24. DIM SUM SIU MAI (PORK DUMPLINGS)

Prep Time: 15 minutes | Cook Time: 12 minutes

Total Time: 27 minutes | Serving: 4

Ingredients

For the filling:

- 1/4 tsp garlic powder
- 1 tbsp chopped green onions
- 1 tbsp soy sauce
- 1 tsp sesame oil
- 1/2 pound ground pork
- 1 tbsp rice vinegar
- 1/4 cup of finely chopped napa cabbage
- 1/2 tsp grated ginger
- 1 tbsp oyster sauce (optional)
- Pinch of white pepper
- Salt to taste

For the wrappers and steaming:

- 24 wonton wrappers
- Parchment paper or silicone steamer mat

Instructions

Get the filling ready:

1. Put chopped napa cabbage, green onions, soy sauce, rice vinegar, oyster sauce (if you want), sesame oil, ginger, garlic powder, white pepper, salt, and soy sauce into a large bowl. Make sure all the ingredients are spread out evenly by mixing them well.
2. In order to put the shumai together, lay a wonton wrapper out on a flat surface. Leave some space around the edges and put a tbsp of filling in the middle.
3. Bring the wrapper's corners together in the middle and pinch them together to make a pouch. You can also make pleats around the sides for a traditional shumai look.
4. Do it again with the rest of the wrappers and filling.
5. Follow the manufacturer's instructions for the shumai and fill your electric steamer with water. Then, bring it to a boil. Use parchment paper or a silicone steamer mat to line the steamer basket.
6. Place the shumai that has been put together so that they don't touch the basket.
7. Steam for 12 to 15 minutes or until the wrappers are clear and the filling is cooked all the way through.
8. To serve, carefully take the shumai out of the steamer and put it on a plate.
9. You can serve it hot with soy sauce, chili oil, hoisin sauce, or any other sauce you like.

VEGETABLES

25. CURRIED CHICKPEA AND VEGGIE BOWLS

Prep Time: 20 minutes | Cook Time: 15 minutes

Total Time: 35 minutes | Serving: 4

Ingredients

For the curried chickpeas:

- 1 tsp ground cumin
- 1/8 tsp cayenne pepper (optional)
- 1/4 tsp ginger powder
- 1/2 tsp turmeric
- 1 tsp ground coriander
- 1/4 tsp garlic powder
- 1 (15 ounce) can chickpeas, drained and rinsed
- 1 tbsp tomato paste
- 1/4 cup of coconut milk (light or full-fat)
- 1/4 tsp chili powder (optional)
- 1/4 cup of vegetable broth
- 1 tbsp olive oil
- Salt and pepper to taste

For the steamed vegetables:

- 1/2 cup of bell pepper, sliced
- 1 cup of chopped sweet potato
- 1 cup of broccoli florets
- 1/2 cup of cherry tomatoes

For the bowls:

- Your favorite toppings (optional): chopped avocado, toasted nuts, yogurt sauce, hot sauce
- Cooked brown rice, quinoa, or other whole grain
- Chopped fresh cilantro (for garnish)
- Lime wedges (for garnish)

Instructions

1. To make the curried chickpeas, mix the cumin, coriander, turmeric, chili powder (if using), ginger powder, garlic powder, and cayenne pepper along with the olive oil in a small bowl.
2. Set a big pot on medium heat. Put the spice mix and stir constantly for 30 seconds, until the food smells good.
3. Put the vegetable broth, tomato paste, coconut milk, and drained chickpeas in the saucepan. Mix everything together, then bring it to a simmer.
4. Turn down the heat and let it simmer for 10 minutes, or until the sauce gets a little thicker and the chickpeas are warm. Add pepper and salt to taste.
5. Steam the vegetables. While the chickpeas are cooking, follow the directions on the package to fill your electric steamer with water and bring it to a boil. Use parchment paper or a silicone steamer mat to line the steamer basket.

6. Put the sweet potato, bell pepper, broccoli florets, and cherry tomatoes in the steamer basket.
7. Steam the vegetables for 8 to 10 minutes, or until they are soft but still crisp.

Put the bowls together:

1. Put cooked brown rice, quinoa, or another whole grain into each of the four bowls.
2. You can put some of the curried chickpeas on top of each bowl.
3. The steamed vegetables should be put on top of the chickpeas.
4. Put lime wedges and chopped cilantro on top.
5. If you want, you can top it with your favorite things, like chopped avocado, toasted nuts, yogurt sauce, or hot sauce.

26. ASIAN VEGETABLE SPRING ROLLS

Prep Time: 20 minutes | Cook Time: 15 minutes

Total Time: 35 minutes | Serving: 4

Ingredients

For the spring rolls:

- 1/4 cup of shredded napa cabbage
- 12 rice paper wrappers
- 1/4 cup of chopped bell pepper
- 1 tbsp rice vinegar
- 1/4 cup of fresh herbs
- 1 tsp sesame oil
- 1/2 cup of shredded cucumber
- 1 tbsp soy sauce
- 1/4 cup of chopped green onions
- 1 cup of shredded carrots
- Salt and pepper to taste

For steaming:

- Parchment paper or silicone steamer matInstructions

Get the filling ready:

1. Mix the chopped carrots, cucumber, green onions, bell pepper, napa cabbage, and fresh herbs in a large bowl.
2. Mix soy sauce, rice vinegar, sesame oil, salt, and pepper in a different bowl using a whisk.
3. The dressing should be poured over the vegetables and mixed together.
4. Put the spring rolls together and steam them:
5. Put warm water in a big bowl. A 15-second soak in water should be enough to make one rice paper wrapper soft but not wet.
6. Place the warmed wrapper flat on a plate. Put some of the fillings close to the bottom edge of the wrapper.
7. Put the filling inside the wrapper and fold the bottom edge over it. Next, tuck the sides of the wrapper very close together. Roll the wrapper up so that it completely covers the filling. Do it again with the rest of the wrappers and filling.
8. Follow the directions on the package to fill your electric steamer with water and then bring it to a boil. Use parchment paper or a silicone steamer mat to line the steamer basket. Place the spring rolls in the basket so that they don't touch each other.
9. For 10 to 12 minutes, or until the filling is hot all the way through and the rice paper wrappers clear up, steam the food.

Serve:

1. Carefully take the spring rolls out of the steamer and put them on a plate.
2. If you want to dip it in something, you can use soy sauce, chili oil, or peanut sauce. Serve it hot.

27. SPICY ASIAN BROCCOLI

Prep Time: 10 minutes | Cook Time: 5-7 minutes

Total Time: 15-17 minutes | Serving: 2-3

Ingredients

- 1 tbsp sesame oil
- 1 tsp sriracha (adjust to your spice preference)
- 1 tbsp rice vinegar
- 1/2 tsp grated ginger
- 1 tbsp soy sauce
- 1 clove garlic, minced
- 1 head of broccoli, cut into florets
- 1/2 tsp sesame seeds (for garnish, optional)
- Pinch of red pepper flakes (optional, for extra heat)

Instructions

1. Get the broccoli ready: Remove the broccoli from the stem and cut it into small florets. Throw away the tough stems.
2. Put the sauce together: Take a small bowl and mix the soy sauce, garlic, rice vinegar, sriracha, ginger, sesame oil, and red pepper flakes if you want to use them.
3. Make the broccoli steam: Follow the directions on the package to fill your electric steamer with water and then bring it to a boil. Use parchment paper or a silicone steamer mat to line the steamer basket.
4. Put in the broccoli: Cover the broccoli and put the florets in the steamer basket.
5. Season and steam: Steam the broccoli for 5 to 7 minutes or until soft but still crisp. After steaming the broccoli, drizzle it with the sauce you made immediately.
6. Add a garnish and serve: Move the broccoli from the steamer to a plate for serving. If you need, you can sprinkle sesame seeds on top. As a side dish, serve it hot or eat it right away.

28. LEMON-GARLIC BRUSSELS SPROUTS

Prep Time: 10 minutes | Cook Time: 7-10 minutes

Total Time: 17-20 minutes | Serving: 4

Ingredients

- 1 pound Brussels sprouts, trimmed and halved
- 1 tbsp olive oil
- 1 tbsp lemon juice
- 1/2 tsp grated garlic
- 1/4 tsp salt
- Pinch of black pepper
- Freshly chopped parsley (optional, for garnish)

Instructions

1. Start by getting the Brussels sprouts ready. Wash them and cut off any tough ends. If they are big, cut them in half lengthwise or into fours.
2. Warm up the steamer: Follow the directions on the package to fill your electric steamer with water and then bring it to a boil. Use parchment paper or a silicone steamer mat to line the steamer basket.
3. Mix the seasonings: Mix the lemon juice, garlic grate, salt, and pepper in a small bowl with a whisk.
4. Toss and steam: Mix the spices together and toss the Brussels sprouts with them until they are evenly covered. Make sure they don't touch too much as you put them in the steamer basket.
5. Season and steam: Steam the Brussels sprouts for 7 to 10 minutes, or until they are just the right amount of soft and crunchy.
6. To serve and decorate, carefully take the Brussels sprouts out of the steamer and put them on a serving dish. If you need, you can add chopped parsley as a garnish. Enjoy while hot!

29. HONEY-SRIRACHA CAULIFLOWER BITES

Prep Time: 15 minutes | Cook Time: 12-15 minutes

Total Time: 27-30 minutes | Serving: 4

Ingredients

For the cauliflower bites:

- 1 head of cauliflower, cut into florets
- 1 tbsp olive oil
- 1/4 tsp salt
- 1/4 tsp black pepper

For the sauce:

- 1 tbsp cornstarch (mixed with 1 tbsp water)
- 1 tbsp sesame oil
- 1 tbsp sriracha
- 1 tbsp rice vinegar
- 2 tbsp honey
- 1/4 cup of soy sauce
- 1 clove garlic, minced
- 1/2 tsp grated ginger

For serving (optional):

- Sesame seeds
- Chopped green onions

Instructions

Get the cauliflower ready:

1. Wash the cauliflower and cut it into florets that are easy to eat. Throw away the tough stems.
2. Follow the directions that came with your electric steamer to heat it.
3. Put in a tiny bowl of soy sauce, honey, sriracha, ginger, rice vinegar, sesame oil, and garlic. Mix them together with a whisk.
4. Make a slurry with cornstarch and one tbsp of water in a different small bowl.
5. Put the cornstarch slurry into the sauce mixture and mix it well with a whisk.
6. Put the cauliflower florets in a bowl and season them with salt and pepper. Then, steam them.
7. Place the cauliflower florets that have been seasoned in the steamer basket so that they don't touch each other too much.
8. Steam for 12 to 15 minutes or until crisp and tender.

Put together and serve:

1. Move the cauliflower florets that have been steamed to a bowl for serving.
2. Pour the ready-made sauce over the cauliflower and gently toss to cover every piece.
3. If you need, you can add sesame seeds and chopped green onions as a garnish.
4. Enjoy while hot!

30. GARLIC HERB GREEN BEANS

Prep Time: 5 minutes | Cook Time: 5-7 minutes

Total Time: 10-12 minutes | Serving: 2-3

Ingredients

- 1/4 tsp dried thyme
- 1/2 tsp minced garlic
- 1/4 tsp dried oregano
- 1 pound fresh green beans, trimmed and washed
- 1 tbsp olive oil
- Pinch of salt and pepper
- Water for steaming

Instructions

1. Get the green beans ready: Clean the green beans and cut off the ends.
2. Warm up the steamer: Follow the directions on the package to fill your electric steamer with water and then bring it to a boil. Use parchment paper or a silicone steamer mat to line the steamer basket.
3. Prepare the seasoning: Olive oil, minced garlic, thyme, oregano, salt, and pepper should all be mixed in a small bowl.
4. Toss and steam: Mix the seasonings and toss the green beans until they are evenly covered. Ensure they don't touch too much as you put them in the steamer basket.
5. Season and steam: Steam the green beans for 5 to 7 minutes or until you like them soft and crisp.
6. To serve, carefully remove the steamer's green beans and put them on a dish. Enjoy while hot!

31. MEDITERRANEAN STUFFED PEPPERS

Prep Time: 20 minutes | Cook Time: 20-25 minutes

Total Time: 40-45 minutes | Serving: 4

Ingredients

For the stuffing:

- 1/2 cup of diced zucchini
- 1/4 cup of crumbled feta cheese
- 1/4 cup of chopped Kalamata olives, pitted
- 1/4 cup of chopped sun-dried tomatoes (oil-packed, drained)
- 1 tbsp olive oil
- 1 cup of cooked brown rice or quinoa
- 1 tbsp chopped fresh mint
- 1/4 tsp salt
- 1/2 onion, finely chopped
- 1/2 cup of chopped bell pepper
- 1/2 tsp dried oregano
- 2 tbsp chopped fresh parsley
- 1 clove garlic, minced
- Pinch of black pepper

For the peppers and steaming:

- 4 bell peppers (red, yellow, orange, or green), tops removed and seeds discarded
- Water for steaming

Instructions

1. Warm up a big pan with olive oil over medium-low heat. Please put in the onion and cook for about 5 minutes until it softens. Put the garlic and cook for one more minute.
2. Dice the zucchini, bell pepper, sun-dried tomatoes, olives, and feta cheese. Add cooked brown rice or quinoa on top. Combine everything, then cook for three to four minutes until hot.
3. Take it off the heat and add the oregano, salt, pepper, parsley, and mint.
4. Fill and steam the peppers: Follow the manufacturer's instructions for heating your electric steamer.
5. Place the bell peppers that have been prepared upright in the steamer basket.
6. Spread the stuffing mixture evenly in the peppers, ensuring they are not too full.
7. Follow the directions to fill your steamer with water and then bring it to a boil.
8. The peppers should be steamed for 20 to 25 minutes or until they are soft and the filling is hot.
9. To serve, carefully take the peppers out of the steamer and put them on plates.
10. If you want, you can drizzle the dish with juices still in the steamer basket's bottom.
11. Have it hot or warm!

32. RAINBOW VEGGIE MEDLEY

Prep Time: 10 minutes | Cook Time: 10-12 minutes

Total Time: 20-22 minutes | Serving: 2-3

Ingredients

- 1/2 tsp dried oregano
- 1/4 tsp garlic powder
- 1/2 cup of red onion, thinly sliced
- 1 cup of sugar snap peas
- 1/4 cup of sliced radishes (optional)
- 1 cup of yellow or red bell pepper, sliced
- 1 cup of baby carrots, halved or quartered if large
- 1 tbsp olive oil
- 1 cup of broccoli florets
- Pinch of salt and pepper
- Fresh herbs for garnish (optional): parsley, dill, chives

Instructions

Get the vegetables ready:

- Clean and cut up all the vegetables. For even cooking, cut them into bite-sized pieces that are all about the same size.
- To season the vegetables, put the cooked vegetables, olive oil, salt, oregano, garlic powder, and pepper in a large bowl. Add toss to cover evenly.
- To steam the vegetables, follow the directions on the package and fill your electric steamer with water. Then, bring it to a boil. Use parchment paper or a silicone steamer mat to line the steamer basket.
- Place the seasoned vegetables in the steamer basket so that they don't touch each other too much.
- Steam the vegetables for 10-12 minutes, or until they are just the right amount of soft and crisp. To find out, you can use a fork to poke them.
- To serve and decorate, carefully take the vegetables out of the steamer and put them on a serving dish.
- If you need, you can add fresh herbs like parsley, dill, or chives as a garnish.
- Enjoy while hot!

33. GARLIC SCAPE AND TOMATO BRUSCHETTA

Prep Time: 15 minutes | Cook Time: 10-12 minutes

Total Time: 25-27 minutes | Serving: 4

Ingredients

For the garlic scape topping:

- 1 tbsp balsamic vinegar
- 1 tbsp olive oil
- 1/2 cup of cherry tomatoes, halved
- 1/2 tsp dried oregano
- 1/4 cup of chopped fresh basil
- 1/4 cup of chopped red onion
- 1 cup of garlic scapes, chopped (flower buds optional, remove tough ends)
- Pinch of salt and pepper

For the bruschetta:

- 1 garlic clove, halved
- 1 baguette, sliced into 1/2-inch thick slices
- 2 tbsp olive oil

Instructions

1. The olive oil should be heated in a pan over medium heat. This will help you make the garlic scape topping. Please put in the chopped garlic scapes and cook for three to four minutes until they get soft and smell good.
2. Olives, red onion, and basil should be added. It should be cooked for two or three more minutes until the tomatoes soften.
3. Taking it off the heat, add the oregano, salt, pepper, and balsamic vinegar and mix them in.

Get the bruschetta ready:

1. Follow the directions that came with your electric steamer to heat it.
2. Dot or brush olive oil on slices of bread. In the steamer basket, toast the bread slices for 5 to 7 minutes or until they are crispy and lightly golden brown.
3. Rub the halved garlic clove to make the toast taste even better.

Put together and serve:

1. Put some ready-made garlic scape and tomato mixture on top of each toasted piece of bread.
2. Serve right away and enjoy!

34. HONEY GLAZED CARROTS

Prep Time: 5 minutes | Cook Time: 8-10 minutes

Total Time: 13-15 minutes | Serving: 4

Ingredients

- 1 tbsp olive oil
- 1 pound carrots, peeled and trimmed
- 2 tbsp honey
- 1 tbsp water
- 1/2 tsp Dijon mustard (optional)
- 1/4 tsp dried thyme (optional)
- Pinch of salt and black pepper

Instructions

1. Get the carrots ready: Remove the carrot peels. Cut them into pieces about the same size, like rounds, sticks, or baby carrots. Little pieces will cook more quickly.
2. Warm up the steamer: Follow the directions on the package to fill your electric steamer with water and then bring it to a boil. Use parchment paper or a silicone steamer mat to line the steamer basket.
3. How to make the glaze: Put olive oil, honey, water, Dijon mustard (if using), thyme (if using), salt, and pepper in a tiny bowl. Set it aside.
4. To steam the carrots, put the carrots that have been cut up into the steamer basket. Spread the carrots out so that they are covered evenly with the honey glaze.
5. Steam and glaze: For 8 to 10 minutes, or until the carrots are soft and crisp to your liking, steam them. To find out, you can use a fork to poke them.
6. Carefully take the carrots out of the steamer and put them on a serving dish. Pour any glaze that's still in the bottom of the steamer basket over the carrots.

35. ROASTED ROOT VEGETABLE MEDLEY

Prep Time: 15 minutes | Cook Time: 20-25 minutes

Total Time: 35-40 minutes | Serving: 4

Ingredients

- 1 tbsp olive oil
- 1 pound assorted root vegetables, peeled and cut into roughly similar-sized pieces
- 1/2 tsp dried thyme
- 1/4 tsp dried rosemary
- Pinch of salt and black pepper
- Optional toppings: chopped fresh herbs (parsley, cilantro, etc.), balsamic glaze, toasted nuts

Instructions

1. Prepare the vegetables: Clean the roots, peel them, and cut them into bite-sized pieces that are all about the same size. This keeps the cooking even all the way through.
2. Warm up the steamer: Follow the directions on the package to fill your electric steamer with water and then bring it to a boil. Use parchment paper or a silicone steamer mat to line the steamer basket.
3. Spice up the vegetables: Olive oil, thyme, rosemary, salt, and pepper should be mixed with the cooked vegetables in a large bowl. Make sure the coating is even on all the pieces.
4. To steam or roast, put the vegetables that have been seasoned in the steamer basket, making sure they don't touch. Soak for 15 to 20 minutes or until the potatoes are soft and crisp to your liking. To find out, you can use a fork to poke them.
5. To serve, carefully remove the steamer's vegetables and put them on a serving dish. You can eat them already browned and caramelized or roast them one more time.

36. ROASTED BUTTERNUT SQUASH WITH SAGE

Prep Time: 10 minutes | Cook Time: 25-30 minutes

Total Time: 35-40 minutes | Serving: 4

Ingredients

- 1/4 tsp black pepper
- 1/4 tsp salt
- 1 tbsp olive oil
- 1/2 tsp dried sage
- 1 small butternut squash (about 2 pounds), peeled and halved lengthwise
- 1/4 cup of grated Parmesan cheese (optional)
- Fresh sage leaves (for garnish, optional)

Instructions

1. Warm the oven up to 400°F (200°C) and get the squash ready. Cut the butternut squash in half lengthwise, remove the seeds, and then cut each half into slices that are 1 inch thick.
2. Warm up the steamer: While the oven heats up, follow the manufacturer's instructions and fill your electric steamer with water. Then, bring it to a boil. Use parchment paper or a silicone steamer mat to line the steamer basket.
3. Put the squash slices in the steamer basket, making sure they don't touch each other too much. Steam for 10 to 15 minutes or until the potatoes are soft but not mushy.
4. Season the squash and roast it. Carefully take it out of the steamer and put it on a baking sheet. Add salt, pepper, and olive oil. Then sprinkle with dried sage. Add toss to cover evenly.
5. Roast and decorate: Put the vegetables in a hot oven and roast them for 15 to 20 minutes, or until they are soft and the edges are starting to turn brown. To get an even browning, flip the squash over halfway through roasting.
6. Serve: Before serving, you may sprinkle with grated Parmesan cheese and fresh sage leaves, but you don't have to. Enjoy!

HEALTHY TWISTS

37. RAINBOW VEGGIE SPRING ROLLS

Prep Time: 20 minutes | Cook Time: 8-10 minutes

Total Time: 28-30 minutes | Serving: 4

Ingredients

For the spring rolls:

- 1/4 cup of shredded napa cabbage
- 1 tbsp soy sauce
- 1/4 cup of chopped green onions
- 1 tsp sesame oil
- 1 cup of shredded carrots
- 1 tbsp rice vinegar
- 1/2 cup of shredded cucumber
- 12 rice paper wrappers
- 1/4 cup of bell pepper
- 1/4 cup of fresh herbs
- Salt and pepper to taste

For steaming:

- Parchment paper or silicone steamer mat

Instructions

Get the filling ready:

1. Mix the chopped carrots, cucumber, green onions, bell pepper, napa cabbage, and fresh herbs in a large bowl.
2. Mix soy sauce, rice vinegar, sesame oil, salt, and pepper in a different bowl using a whisk. The dressing should be poured over the vegetables and mixed.
3. Fill a large bowl with warm water to make the spring rolls and steam them. A 15-second soak in water should make one rice paper wrapper soft but not wet.
4. Place the warmed wrapper flat on a plate. Put some of the fillings close to the bottom edge of the wrapper.
5. Put the filling inside the wrapper and fold the bottom edge over it. Next, tuck the sides of the wrapper very close together. Roll the wrapper up so that it completely covers the filling. Do it again with the rest of the wrappers and filling.
6. Follow the manufacturer's instructions for steaming and fill your electric steamer with water. Then, bring it to a boil. Use parchment paper or a silicone steamer mat to line the steamer basket. Place the spring rolls in the basket so they don't touch each other.
7. Steam the food for 8 to 10 minutes, or until the filling is hot all the way through and the rice paper wrappers clear up.
8. To serve, carefully take the spring rolls out of the steamer and put them on a plate.
9. If you want to dip it in something, you can use soy sauce, chili oil, or peanut sauce. Serve it hot.

38. KOREAN-INSPIRED STEAMED CHICKEN WRAPS

Prep Time: 20 minutes | Cook Time: 15 minutes

Total Time: 35 minutes | Serving: 4

Ingredients

For the chicken:

- 1 tbsp honey
- 1 pound boneless, skinless chicken breasts, thin-sliced
- 1 tbsp grated ginger
- 1/4 tsp black pepper
- 1 tbsp rice vinegar
- 1 tbsp minced garlic
- 2 tbsp soy sauce
- 1 tsp sesame oil
- 1/2 tsp red pepper flakes

For the wraps:

- 8 large lettuce leaves
- 1 cup of cooked white or brown rice
- 1/4 cup of sliced cucumber
- 1/2 cup of shredded carrots
- 1/4 cup of chopped green onions
- 1/4 cup of kimchi (optional)
- Gochujang sauce (for serving)
- Sesame seeds (for garnish, optional)

Instructions

1. To prepare the chicken, put soy sauce, honey, rice vinegar, garlic, ginger, sesame oil, black pepper, and red pepper flakes in a bowl and mix them together. Toss the chicken slices in the sauce to make sure they are evenly covered. Let it sit for at least 15 minutes, or up to 30 minutes if you want it to taste even better.
2. To steam the chicken, follow the directions on the package and fill your electric steamer with water. Then, bring it to a boil. Use parchment paper or a silicone steamer mat to line the steamer basket.
3. Stack the chicken slices that have been marinated on top of each other in the steamer basket.
4. The chicken should be steamed for 10-12 minutes, or until it is fully cooked and no longer pink inside.

Put the wraps together:

1. If you want the lettuce leaves to be more flexible, you can briefly warm them in the steamer. On each lettuce leaf, put some cooked rice.
2. Put shredded carrots, cucumber, green onions, and kimchi on top, if you're using it.
3. Put in chicken slices that have been steamed, and then add gochujang sauce to taste.
4. On top of the filling, fold the bottom of the lettuce leaf up. Then, roll up the sides to make a wrap.
5. If you need, you can sprinkle sesame seeds on top and serve right away.

39. STEAMED CHICKEN AND VEGETABLE PAD THAI

Prep Time: 20 minutes | Cook Time: 15-20 minutes

Total Time: 35-40 minutes | Serving: 4

Ingredients

For the chicken:

- 1/2 tsp garlic powder
- 1 tsp grated ginger
- 1 tbsp soy sauce
- 1 tbsp brown sugar
- 1/4 tsp black pepper
- 1 pound boneless, skinless chicken breasts, thinly sliced
- 1 tbsp fish sauce (optional)

For the vegetables:

- 1/4 cup of mung bean sprouts
- 1/4 cup of chopped green onions
- 1 cup of rice noodles (thin or pad thai noodles)
- 1 cup of shredded carrots
- 1/2 cup of sliced bell peppers (various colors)

For the sauce:

- 1 tbsp lime juice
- 1 tbsp brown sugar
- 2 tbsp soy sauce
- 2 tbsp tamarind paste
- 1/2 tsp chili flakes
- 1 tbsp fish sauce (optional)
- 1 tbsp water

For serving:

- Chopped peanuts
- Fresh cilantro or lime wedges (optional)

Instructions

1. To prepare the chicken, mix soy sauce, brown sugar, ginger, garlic powder, fish sauce (if using), and black pepper in a bowl. Toss the chicken slices in the sauce to make sure they are evenly covered. Let it sit for at least 15 minutes, or up to 30 minutes if you want it to taste even better.
2. To steam the chicken and vegetables, follow the directions on the package and fill your electric steamer with water. Then, bring it to a boil. Stack the chicken slices one on top of the other in the steamer basket.
3. The chicken should be steamed for 5 to 7 minutes, or until it is fully cooked and no longer pink inside.
4. Place the rice noodles on top of the chicken in the steamer basket. For another three to five minutes, or until the noodles are soft and clear, steam them again.
5. Shred the carrots, bell peppers, and mung bean sprouts and put them in the steamer basket. For another two to three minutes, or until the vegetables are soft but still crisp, steam them again.
6. Set the sauce aside while the chicken and vegetables steam. In a small dish, mix the tamarind paste, soy sauce, lime juice, water, brown sugar, chili flakes, and fish sauce (if using).

Put together and serve:

1. Place the steamed chicken, noodles, and vegetables on plates to serve.
2. Pour the ready-made sauce over the food and toss it around to cover it all.
3. You can add chopped peanuts, fresh cilantro, or lime wedges as a garnish.

40. SPICY TOFU AND EDAMAME LETTUCE WRAPS

Prep Time: 20 minutes | Cook Time: 15-20 minutes

Total Time: 35-40 minutes | Serving: 4

Ingredients

For the chicken:

- 1 pound boneless, skinless chicken breasts, thinly sliced
- 1/2 tsp garlic powder
- 1/4 tsp black pepper
- 1 tbsp fish sauce (optional)
- 1 tsp grated ginger
- 1 tbsp soy sauce
- 1 tbsp brown sugar

For the vegetables:

- 1/2 cup of sliced bell peppers (various colors)
- 1 cup of rice noodles (thin or pad thai noodles)
- 1/4 cup of mung bean sprouts
- 1/4 cup of chopped green onions
- 1 cup of shredded carrots

For the sauce:

- 1/2 tsp chili flakes (adjust to your preference)
- 1 tbsp water
- 1 tbsp brown sugar
- 2 tbsp soy sauce
- 1 tbsp lime juice
- 2 tbsp tamarind paste
- 1 tbsp fish sauce (optional)

For serving:

- Chopped peanuts
- Fresh cilantro or lime wedges (optional)

Instructions

1. To prepare the chicken, mix soy sauce, brown sugar, ginger, garlic powder, fish sauce (if using), and black pepper in a bowl. Toss the chicken slices in the sauce to make sure they are evenly covered. Let it sit for at least 15 minutes or up to 30 minutes if you want it to taste even better.
2. To steam the chicken and vegetables, follow the directions on the package and fill your electric steamer with water. Then, bring it to a boil. Stack the chicken slices one on top of the other in the steamer basket.
3. The chicken should be steamed for 5 to 7 minutes or until it is fully cooked and no longer pink inside.
4. Place the rice noodles on top of the chicken in the steamer basket. For another three to five minutes, or until the noodles are soft and clear, steam them again.
5. Shred the carrots, bell peppers, and mung bean sprouts and put them in the steamer basket. For another two to three minutes, or until the vegetables are soft but still crisp, steam them again.
6. Set the sauce aside while the chicken and vegetables steam. In a small dish, mix the tamarind paste, soy sauce, lime juice, water, brown sugar, chili flakes, and fish sauce (if using).

Put together and serve:

1. Place the steamed chicken, noodles, and vegetables on plates to serve.
2. Pour the ready-made sauce over the food and toss it around to cover it all.
3. You can add chopped peanuts, fresh cilantro, or lime wedges as a garnish.

41. SALMON WITH LEMONY ASPARAGUS AND QUINOA

Prep Time: 10 minutes | Cook Time: 15-20 minutes

Total Time: 25-30 minutes | Serving: 2

Ingredients

For the salmon:

- 1/4 tsp garlic powder
- 2 salmon fillets (6-8 ounce each)
- 1 tbsp olive oil
- 1/2 tsp dried dill
- Salt and pepper to taste

For the asparagus:

- 12-15 asparagus spears, trimmed
- 1/2 tsp olive oil
- 1 tbsp lemon juice
- Salt and pepper to taste

For the quinoa:

- 1 cup of cooked quinoa
- 1/4 cup of chopped fresh parsley

Instructions

Get the salmon ready:

1. Follow the directions that came with your electric steamer to heat it up.
2. Wet the salmon fillets with paper towels and pat them dry. Mix olive oil, dill, garlic powder, salt, and pepper in a small dish with a whisk. Use the mix to brush the salmon fillets.

Get the asparagus ready:

1. Put salt, pepper, lemon juice, and olive oil to the asparagus spears and toss them around.
2. Steam the salmon and asparagus. In the steamer basket, lay out the asparagus spears in a single layer. After the asparagus, put the salmon fillets on top of it.
3. Steam the salmon and asparagus for 12 to 15 minutes, or until the salmon is cooked through and the asparagus is soft but crisp.

Put together and serve:

1. Put some cooked quinoa on each of two plates. The steamed salmon and asparagus should be put on top.
2. Add some chopped fresh parsley on top and enjoy!

42. SPICY CHIPOTLE BLACK BEAN BURGERS

Prep Time: 15 minutes | Cook Time: 12-15 minutes

Total Time: 27-30 minutes | Serving: 4

Ingredients

- 1 tbsp chipotle pepper in adobo sauce, finely chopped
- 1/4 cup of finely chopped red onion
- 1/4 cup of chopped bell pepper
- 15 ounce can black beans, drained and rinsed
- 1/2 cup of cooked brown rice
- 1 tbsp olive oil
- 1/4 tsp smoked paprika
- 1 tsp ground cumin
- 1/2 tsp garlic powder
- 1 tbsp chopped cilantro
- 1/4 cup of bread crumbs (optional)
- Salt and pepper to taste
- Cooking spray

Instructions

1. Prepare ingredients: In a big bowl, use a fork to mash the black beans. You could also pulse them a few times in a food processor to make them a little chunkier.
2. Blend the black beans with olive oil, cumin, garlic powder, smoked paprika, salt, and pepper. Then add the red onion, bell pepper, cilantro, and cooked brown rice. Combine well by mixing.
3. The step you can skip: If the mixture seems too wet, add the breadcrumbs little by little, mixing after each addition until the mixture is the right consistency for making patties.
4. Make the patties into: Make firm patties out of each of the four equal parts of the mixture.
5. Warm up your electric steamer: Follow the directions on the package to fill the steamer with water and then bring it to a boil. Use parchment paper or a silicone steamer mat to line the steamer basket.
6. Spray cooking spray on the steamer basket before putting the burgers in it. Make sure the patties don't touch each other as you put them in the basket.
7. For 12 to 15 minutes, or until the burgers are hot all the way through and feel firm when you touch them, steam them. Stick a toothpick into the middle to see if it's done; it should come out clean.

43. CURRIED CARROT AND CHICKPEA FRITTERS

Prep Time: 15 minutes | Cook Time: 12-15 minutes

Total Time: 27-30 minutes | Serving: 4

Ingredients

- 1 tbsp chipotle pepper in adobo sauce, finely chopped
- 1/4 cup of finely chopped red onion
- 1/4 cup of chopped bell pepper
- 15 ounce can black beans, drained and rinsed
- 1/2 cup of cooked brown rice
- 1 tbsp olive oil
- 1/4 tsp smoked paprika
- 1 tsp ground cumin
- 1/2 tsp garlic powder
- 1 tbsp chopped cilantro
- 1/4 cup of bread crumbs (optional)
- Salt and pepper to taste
- Cooking spray

Instructions

1. Get the ingredients ready: Cut the red onion and cilantro into small pieces and grate the carrots. Let the chickpeas drain and rinse them.
2. Put the ingredients together: Grate the carrots and add them to a large bowl. Add the chickpeas, salt, red onion, cilantro, olive oil, curry powder, cumin, garlic powder, and pepper. Mix everything together well until it's all mixed in evenly.
3. Make the fritters into: Form the mixture into 8 thin patties that are all the same size. You could also use a spoon to make small fritters that are easy to eat.
4. Warm up your electric steamer: Follow the directions on the package to fill the steamer with water and then bring it to a boil. Use parchment paper or a silicone steamer mat to line the steamer basket.
5. Spray cooking spray on the steamer basket before putting the fritters in it. Make sure the fritters don't touch each other as you put them in the basket.
6. They should be steamed for 12 to 15 minutes or until they are set and cooked all the way through. If you gently press on a fritter, you can tell if it's done. It should feel firm.

44. MANGO AND BLACK BEAN SALSA VERDE

Prep Time: 15 minutes | Cook Time: 20-25 minutes

Total Time: 35-40 minutes | Serving: 4

Ingredients

For the salsa verde:

- 1/4 tsp black pepper
- 2 Jalapenos, seeded and finely chopped
- 1/2 tsp salt
- 1/2 red onion, finely chopped
- 1 mango, peeled and diced
- 1/4 cup of fresh lime juice
- 1/4 cup of chopped fresh cilantro
- 1 (15 ounce) can black beans, drained and rinsed
- 1 tbsp olive oil

For the baked plantain:

- 2 ripe plantains, peeled and sliced diagonally into 1/2-inch thick pieces
- 1/2 tsp ground cumin
- 1 tbsp olive oil
- 1/4 tsp garlic powder
- Pinch of salt

Instructions

1. To make the salsa verde, put the black beans, red onion, cilantro, Jalapenos, olive oil, lime juice, pepper, and salt in a big dish and mix them together. Combine well by mixing. Check the seasonings and make any changes you want.
2. Get the plantain ready to bake:
3. Warm the oven up to 200°C (400°F).
4. Add the vegetable slices to a bowl and add the olive oil, cumin, garlic powder, and salt.
5. Place the plantain slices on a parchment-lined baking sheet so that they can all fit together.
6. Flip the plantains over halfway through baking and bake for another 15 to 20 minutes, or until they are soft and a little golden brown.

Put together and serve:

1. Put some salsa verde in each bowl to serve.
2. Baked plantain slices should be put on top of each serving.
3. You can dip it in pita bread or tortilla chips.

45. LENTIL AND SWEET POTATO SHEPHERD'S PIE

Prep Time: 15 minutes | Cook Time: 25-30 minutes

Total Time: 40-45 minutes | Serving: 4

Ingredients

For the lentil filling:

- 1 tbsp tomato paste
- 1 (14.5 ounce) can diced tomatoes, undrained
- 1 cup of brown lentils, rinsed
- 1 tbsp olive oil
- 2 carrots, peeled and diced
- 1 tsp dried thyme
- 2 cloves garlic, minced
- 2 celery stalks, diced
- 4 cups of vegetable broth
- 1 onion, finely chopped
- 1/2 tsp dried rosemary
- Salt and pepper to taste

For the sweet potato topping:

- 1/4 tsp ground nutmeg
- 2 medium sweet potatoes, peeled and diced
- 1/2 tsp ground cinnamon
- 1 tbsp olive oil
- Salt and pepper to taste

Instructions

1. Warm the olive oil in a big dish or Dutch oven over medium-low heat. This will help you make the lentil filling. Put in the celery, carrots, and onion. Cook for 5 minutes or until the vegetables get soft. After you add the garlic, cook for one more minute.
2. Pour the lentils, vegetable broth, tomato paste, thyme, rosemary, salt, and pepper into the pot. Do not forget to rinse the lentils first. Bring it to a boil, boil it, and let it cook for twenty to twenty-five minutes until the lentils are soft.
3. Make the sweet potato topping while the lentils are cooking: Follow the directions with your electric steamer to heat it. Put the sweet potatoes cut into small pieces in the steamer basket.
4. Put olive oil, cinnamon, nutmeg, salt, and pepper in a small bowl. Spoon the mix over the sweet potatoes and mix them around to cover them all.
5. Cook the sweet potatoes in water: Steam for 15 to 20 minutes or until soft and a fork can go through them quickly.
6. Put the shepherd's pie together: Warm the oven up to 375°F (190°C) after the lentils and sweet potatoes are done. Put the lentil mixture in a baking dish. Spread the mashed or roughly mashed sweet potatoes out evenly on top.
7. Bake for 15 to 20 minutes or until the topping is bubbly and golden brown.
8. Serve: Let it cool down a bit before you serve it. Enjoy!

46. STEAMED SHRIMP SCAMPI WITH ZUCCHINI NOODLES

Prep Time: 10 minutes | Cook Time: 10-12 minutes

Total Time: 20-22 minutes | Serving: 2

Ingredients

- 1 pound medium shrimp, peeled and deveined
- 1 tbsp olive oil
- 1/4 cup of lemon juice
- 2 medium zucchini, spiralized into noodles (zoodles)
- 1 tbsp chopped fresh parsley
- 2 cloves garlic, minced
- 1/4 cup of dry white wine or chicken broth
- 1 tbsp butter (optional)
- 1/4 tsp red pepper flakes (optional)
- Salt and pepper to taste
- Fresh lemon wedges, for serving

Instructions

1. To make the shrimp, put them in a small bowl and put 1 tbsp of olive oil, salt, and pepper. Toss the shrimp to coat them.
2. Warm up your electric steamer: Follow the directions on the package to fill the steamer with water and then bring it to a boil. Use parchment paper or a silicone steamer mat to line the steamer basket. This will make it easier to clean up.
3. Season the shrimp and put them in the steamer basket. Steam for 5 to 7 minutes or until the shrimp is pink and cooked all the way through.
4. As the shrimp steers, prepare the sauce. Use medium-low heat to heat the rest of the olive oil in a large skillet, along with the garlic and red pepper flakes. For 30 seconds, cook until the food smells good.
5. Clean out the pan: You can use chicken broth or white wine. Make sure to scrape the bottom of the pan to get these browned bits. Allow to simmer for one minute to slightly lower the heat.
6. Put the sauce away: Salt and pepper should be added along with the lemon juice.
7. After the shrimp are done cooking, add the zoodles to the pan and toss them in the sauce for one to two minutes to heat them through.
8. Put everything together: Toss the cooked shrimp back into the pan with the rest of the food to coat.
9. Serve: Put the shrimp scampi on plates right away to be served. Put some drops of fresh lemon juice on top and enjoy!

47. SPICY SWEET POTATO AND BLACK BEAN TACOS

Prep Time: 15 minutes | Cook Time: 20-25 minutes

Total Time: 35-40 minutes | Serving: 4

Ingredients

For the sweet potato filling:

- 1/4 tsp smoked paprika
- 2 medium sweet potatoes, peeled and diced
- 1 tbsp olive oil
- Salt and pepper to taste
- 1/2 tsp ground cumin
- 1/4 tsp chili powder
- Pinch of cayenne pepper

For the black bean mixture:

- 1/2 red onion, finely chopped
- 1/2 tsp ground cumin
- 1/4 tsp chili powder
- 1 (15 ounce) can black beans, drained and rinsed
- 1 Jalapeno, seeded and finely chopped
- 1 clove garlic, minced
- 1 tbsp lime juice
- 1/4 cup of chopped fresh cilantro
- Salt and pepper to taste

For the tacos:

- 8 small corn tortillas
- Chopped red onion (optional)
- Chopped avocado (optional)
- Fresh cilantro (optional)
- Hot sauce (optional)
- Lime wedges (optional)

Instructions

Prepare the sweet potato filling:

1. Follow the directions that came with your electric steamer to heat it up. Put the sweet potatoes that have been cut into small pieces in the steamer basket.
2. Put olive oil, cumin, smoked paprika, chili powder, salt, pepper, and cayenne pepper (if being used) in a small bowl. Spoon the mix over the sweet potatoes and mix them around to cover them all.
3. After 15 to 20 minutes of steaming, the sweet potatoes should be soft enough that a fork can easily go through them.

Prepare the black bean mixture:

1. While the sweet potatoes are steaming, use a fork to mash the black beans in a bowl or pulse them a few times in a food processor to make them a little chunkier.

2. Mix in the cilantro, lime juice, cumin, chili powder, salt, and pepper. You may also add the Jalapeno if you're using it. Combine well by mixing. Put the tacos together:
3. Following the directions on the package, warm the tortillas.
4. Spread the black bean and sweet potato filling out evenly on each tortilla.
5. You can add chopped avocado, red onion, cilantro, lime wedges, hot sauce, or anything else you like on top.
6. Enjoy!

48. TURMERIC CAULIFLOWER RICE BUDDHA BOWL

Prep Time: 15 minutes | Cook Time: 20-25 minutes

Total Time: 35-40 minutes | Serving: 2

Ingredients

For the turmeric cauliflower rice:

- 1 tsp turmeric powder
- 1/2 tsp ground cumin
- 1 tbsp olive oil
- 1 head cauliflower, trimmed and florets chopped
- 1/4 tsp garlic powder
- Salt and pepper to taste

For the other components:

- 1/4 cup of sliced red onion
- 1/4 cup of chopped avocado
- 1/4 cup of chopped fresh cilantro
- 1/2 cup of roasted sweet potato cubes
- 1 cup of cooked chickpeas, drained and rinsed
- 1 tbsp tahini dressing
- 1/4 cup of chopped cucumber
- Lime wedges, for serving
- Optional toppings: crumbled tempeh, sriracha mayo, toasted nuts, seeds

Tahini Dressing:

- 1 clove garlic, minced
- 1 tbsp water
- Pinch of red pepper flakes
- 1 tbsp olive oil
- 2 tbsp soy sauce (or tamari for gluten-free)
- 1 tbsp rice vinegar
- 1/2 tsp ginger, grated
- 2 tbsp tahini

Instructions

Prepare the turmeric cauliflower rice:

1. Follow the directions that came with your electric steamer to heat it up.
2. The cauliflower florets, olive oil, cumin, garlic powder, salt, and pepper should all be mixed together in a large bowl. Add toss to cover evenly.
3. Put the cauliflower florets that have been seasoned in the steamer basket.
4. Steam the cauliflower for 15-20 minutes, or until it's soft and fully cooked.

Prepare the other components:

1. Put the sweet potato cubes in the oven at 400°Fahrenheit (200°C) for 20-25 minutes or until soft and lightly browned. Do this while the cauliflower is steaming.
2. Cut the avocado, cucumber, and red onion into thin slices.
3. In a small bowl, mix the tahini dressing ingredients with a whisk until the dressing is smooth.

Assemble the buddha bowls:

1. Put some of the cooked cauliflower rice in each bowl.
2. Red onion, cucumber, avocado, roasted sweet potato cubes, and fresh cilantro should be put on top.
3. Add as much tahini dressing as you like.
4. You can add lime wedges and any other toppings you like on top.

SIDE DISHES

49. GARLIC HERB GREEN BEANS

Prep Time: 5 minutes | Cook Time: 10 minutes

Total Time: 15 minutes | Servings: 4

Ingredients

- 2 cloves garlic, minced
- 1 tbsp olive oil
- 1 pound fresh green beans, trimmed and washed
- 1/2 tsp dried thyme
- 1/4 cup of sliced almonds, toasted
- 1/4 tsp dried oregano
- Salt and freshly ground black pepper, to taste

Instructions

1. Follow the directions that came with your electric steamer to add water. Heat the water.
2. Dry out a skillet and set it over medium-low heat. Toast the almonds for about 5 minutes or until they turn golden brown. Do this while the water heats up. Put away.
3. Add the garlic, thyme, oregano, salt, and pepper to the green beans in a large bowl. Toss the beans to coat them.
4. In a steamer basket, put the green beans. Steam them for 5 to 7 minutes or until they are crisp-tender.
5. After the green beans are steamed, put them on a serving dish and add the toasted almonds. Have fun, hot!

50. GARLIC SCAPE AND TOMATO BRUSCHETTA

Prep Time: 10 minutes | Cook Time: 12 minutes

Total Time: 22 minutes | Servings: 4

Ingredients

- 1/2 tsp dried oregano
- 1/4 cup of red onion, finely diced
- 1 bunch garlic scapes, trimmed and cut into 1-inch pieces
- 2 medium tomatoes, seeded and diced
- Salt and freshly ground black pepper, to taste
- 1 tsp balsamic vinegar
- 4 slices crusty bread, toasted
- 1 tbsp olive oil
- Fresh basil leaves, for garnish (optional)

Instructions

1. Follow the directions that came with your electric steamer to add water. Heat the water.
2. Add the tomatoes, salt, red onion, oregano, olive oil, balsamic vinegar, and pepper to a bowl while the water heats up. Toss to cover.
3. Put the ingredients in the steamer basket and steam for 8 to 10 minutes or until the tomatoes and garlic scapes are soft.
4. Use a toaster or a broiler to make the bread golden brown and crisp.
5. Put a lot of the steamed garlic scape and tomato mixture on top of each slice of toast.
6. If you need, you can add fresh basil leaves as a garnish. Enjoy right away!

51. HONEY-GLAZED CARROTS WITH ORANGE ZEST

Prep Time: 5 minutes | Cook Time: 10-12 minutes

Total Time: 15-17 minutes | Servings: 4

Ingredients

- 1/2 orange, zested and juiced
- 2 tbsp honey
- 1 tbsp butter
- 1/4 tsp ground ginger (optional)
- 1 pound baby carrots, trimmed and peeled (optional)
- Salt and freshly ground black pepper, to taste
- Fresh parsley, for garnish (optional)

Instructions

1. Follow the directions that came with your electric steamer to add water. Heat the water up. In a tiny dish, mix the orange zest, orange juice, honey, butter, and ginger (if using) with a whisk while the water heats. Put away.
2. Put the carrots in the steamer basket and steam them for 8 to 10 minutes, or until they are soft but still crisp. After steaming, carefully move the carrots to a dish to serve.
3. The honey-orange glaze should be poured over the carrots and mixed well.
4. Add pepper and salt to taste. If you need, you can add fresh parsley as a garnish. Serve right away.

52. HONEY-SRIRACHA GLAZED BRUSSELS SPROUTS

Prep Time: 5 minutes | Cook Time: 10-12 minutes

Total Time: 15-17 minutes | Servings: 4

Ingredients

- 1 tbsp soy sauce
- 1 pound Brussels sprouts, trimmed and halved or quartered
- 1 tbsp olive oil
- 2 tbsp sriracha sauce
- 1/4 tsp garlic powder
- 2 tbsp honey
- 1/2 tsp sesame oil (optional)
- Salt and freshly ground black pepper, to taste
- Sesame seeds, for garnish (optional)

Instructions

1. Follow the directions that came with your electric steamer to add water. Heat the water.
2. In a tiny bowl, mix the honey, sriracha, soy sauce, olive oil, sesame oil (if using), and garlic powder with a whisk while the water heats up. Put away.
3. Put the Brussels sprouts in the basket of the steamer. Steam them for 8 to 10 minutes or until they are soft but still have some crunch.
4. After steaming, carefully move the Brussels sprouts to a dish to serve.
5. The honey-sriracha glaze should be poured over the Brussels sprouts and mixed well.
6. Add pepper and salt to taste.
7. If you need, you can sprinkle sesame seeds on top. Serve right away.

53. HONEY GLAZED CARROTS WITH PECANS

Prep Time: 5 minutes | Cook Time: 10-12 minutes

Total Time: 15-17 minutes | Servings: 4

Ingredients

- 1/4 tsp Ground cinnamon
- 2 tbsp Butter
- 2 tbsp Honey
- 1/4 cup of Raw pecans, toasted
- 1 pound Baby carrots, trimmed and peeled (optional)
- Salt and freshly ground black pepper to taste
- Fresh parsley, for garnish (optional)

Instructions

1. Follow the directions that came with your electric steamer to add water. Heat the water.
2. Prepare the water by heating it up. Toast the pecans over medium-low heat for about 5 minutes or until they turn golden brown and smell good. Put away.
3. Mix the honey, butter, and cinnamon together in a small bowl. Add pepper and salt to taste.
4. Put the carrots in the steamer basket and steam them for 8 to 10 minutes or until they are soft but still crisp.
5. After steaming, carefully move the carrots to a dish to serve.
6. Sprinkle the carrots with the honey-butter glaze and toss them around to cover them all.
7. Put the pecans that have been toasted on top of the carrots.
8. If you need, you can add fresh parsley as a garnish. Serve right away.

54. MEDITERRANEAN STUFFED PEPPERS

Prep Time: 10 minutes | Cook Time: 15-20 minutes

Total Time: 25-30 minutes | Servings: 4

Ingredients

- 1/4 cup of Chopped red onion
- 1/4 cup of Chopped Kalamata olives
- 2 tbsp Olive oil
- 1 cup of Cooked quinoa
- 1/2 tsp Dried oregano
- 1/2 cup of Crumbled feta cheese
- 4 Bell peppers, any color combination
- 1 tbsp Lemon juice
- 2 tbsp Chopped fresh parsley
- Salt and freshly ground black pepper to taste

Instructions

1. Cut each pepper off the top and remove the seeds and membranes. Wash the peppers and put them in a baking dish so they stand up straight.
2. Add the feta cheese, olives, red onion, parsley, olive oil, lemon juice, oregano, salt, and pepper to a large bowl. Pour the cooked quinoa on top. Combine well.
3. Fill the pepper holes with the quinoa mixture, making sure it fits tightly.
4. Follow the directions that came with your electric steamer to add water. Heat the water up.
5. In a steamer, put the baking dish with the stuffed peppers and steam for 15 to 20 minutes, or until the peppers are soft and the filling is hot.
6. Take the peppers out of the steamer carefully and serve them right away.

55. STEAMED ARTICHOKES WITH LEMON BUTTER DIP

Prep Time: 10 minutes | Cook Time: 30-45 minutes

Total Time: 40-55 minutes | Servings: 4

Ingredients

- 4 Artichokes
- 1 Lemon, cut into wedges

For the lemon butter dip:

- 1/4 tsp Black pepper
- 2 tbsp Fresh lemon juice
- 1/4 tsp Salt
- 1/2 tsp Dried parsley
- 1/2 cup of Unsalted butter, softened

Instructions

1. Follow the directions that came with your electric steamer to add water. Heat the water.
2. Cut each artichoke's stem off by about an inch. Cut off the sharp ends of the leaves with kitchen shears. With a sharp knife, carefully cut off the tough leaves on the outside until you get to the yellow leaves below.
3. Rub the artichokes with a lemon wedge to keep them from turning brown. In a steamer basket, put the artichokes. Put them in the steamer for 30 to 45 minutes or until the leaves are soft enough to pull off.
4. Set the lemon butter dip aside while the artichokes steam. In a small bowl, melt the butter and mix it with the parsley, salt, and pepper.
5. Warm up the artichokes and put them out with the lemon butter dip.

56. RAINBOW VEGGIE MEDLEY WITH QUINOA

Prep Time: 10 minutes | Cook Time: 20 minutes

Total Time: 30 minutes | Servings: 4

Ingredients

- 1/2 cup of baby spinach
- 1 small broccoli head, cut into florets
- 1 red bell pepper, sliced
- 1 orange bell pepper, sliced
- 1/2 tsp salt
- 1 green bell pepper, sliced
- 1/4 tsp black pepper
- 1 cup of quinoa, rinsed
- 1 cup of cherry tomatoes
- 1 yellow bell pepper, sliced
- 1 1/2 cups of water or vegetable broth
- 1 tbsp olive oil
- 1/4 cup of crumbled feta cheese (optional)
- 1/4 cup of chopped fresh parsley (optional)

Instructions

1. Put the quinoa, broth or water, salt, and pepper in the steamer basket.
2. Add the broccoli, cherry tomatoes, and bell peppers to a different bowl and toss them with the olive oil.
3. In the steamer basket, put the vegetables on top of the quinoa.
4. Cover the steamer and steam for as long as your steamer's instructions say to, usually 20 minutes, or until the quinoa is cooked all through and the vegetables are crisp-tender.
5. Fork the quinoa once it's done cooking, and add the spinach. Stir it in until it wilts.
6. You can sprinkle crumbled feta cheese and chopped parsley on top if you want.

57. STEAMED ASPARAGUS WITH BALSAMIC GLAZE

Prep Time: 5 minutes | Cook Time: 10 minutes

Total Time: 15 minutes | Servings: 2

Ingredients

- 1 bunch asparagus, trimmed
- 1 tbsp olive oil
- 1/4 cup of balsamic vinegar
- Salt and pepper to taste
- 1 tbsp brown sugar (optional)

Instructions

- Follow the directions that came with your electric steamer to add water.
- Put the asparagus in the steamer basket and steam it for four to five minutes or until it is soft but still crisp.
- Mix the salt, olive oil, and pepper in a tiny bowl with a whisk while the asparagus cooks.
- Heat the balsamic vinegar over medium-low heat in a different saucepan for about 5 minutes or until it cuts in half and gets a little thicker. If using brown sugar, stir it in and cook for one more minute until it melts.
- Spread the steamed asparagus on a plate and drizzle with the balsamic glaze.
- Serve right away and enjoy!

58. STEAMED SUGAR SNAP PEAS WITH SESAME OIL

Prep Time: 5 minutes | Cook Time: 4-5 minutes

Total Time: 9-10 minutes | Servings: 2

Ingredients

- 1 tbsp toasted sesame oil
- 1/2 tsp sea salt
- 1/4 tsp freshly cracked black pepper
- 1 pound fresh sugar snap peas, strings removed (optional)
- Optional garnishes: Chopped fresh cilantro, sesame seeds, toasted almonds

Instructions

1. Get the peas ready: Sugar snap peas should be washed and trimmed, and any strings should be taken off. If you want, you can leave the strings on for extra fiber.
2. Fill the steamer: Follow the directions on the package to fill your electric steamer with water.
3. As soon as the sugar snap peas are ready, put them in the steamer basket. Cover and steam for 4 to 5 minutes, or until the potatoes are soft and crispy to your liking.
4. Add salt and serve: Put the steamed sugar snap peas in a large bowl. Put the sesame oil on top, then add the salt and pepper. Gently toss to coat.
5. For more flavor and texture, you can put chopped fresh cilantro, sesame seeds, or toasted almonds as a garnish before serving.

59. ASIAN STEAMED BROCCOLI WITH SESAME SAUCE

Prep Time: 5 minutes | Cook Time: 10 minutes

Total Time: 15 minutes | Servings: 2

Ingredients

- 1 tbsp soy sauce
- 1/2 tsp grated ginger
- 1 head broccoli, cut into florets
- 1 tsp sesame oil
- 1 tbsp toasted sesame seeds
- 1 tbsp rice vinegar
- 1 clove garlic, minced
- 1/4 tsp red pepper flakes (optional)

Instructions

1. Get the sauce ready: If you want to use red pepper flakes, mix them with soy sauce, rice vinegar, sesame oil, ginger, and garlic in a small bowl. Put away.
2. Make the broccoli steam: Follow the directions that came with your electric steamer to add water. Put the broccoli florets in the steamer basket and steam them for four to five minutes or until they are soft but still crisp.
3. Throw and serve: Put the steamed broccoli in a large bowl. Stir the broccoli around a few times to coat it with the sesame sauce.
4. Top it off and enjoy: Add toasted sesame seeds on top, and serve right away.

60. SPICY ASIAN EDAMAME PODS

Prep Time: 5 minutes | Cook Time: 10 minutes

Total Time: 15 minutes | Servings: 2

Ingredients

- 1 tbsp toasted sesame oil
- 1 tbsp soy sauce
- 1 tsp minced ginger
- 1 clove garlic, minced
- 1 cup of edamame pods
- 2 tbsp rice vinegar
- 1/4 tsp red pepper flakes (optional)
- Salt and pepper to taste

Instructions

1. Get the seasoning ready: As you like, add red pepper flakes, soy sauce, rice vinegar, sesame oil, ginger, garlic, and salt and pepper to taste in a small bowl. Put away.
2. To steam the edamame: Follow the directions that came with your electric steamer to add water. Put the edamame pods in the steamer basket and steam them for 5 to 6 minutes, or until they turn bright green and get a little soft.
3. Throw and serve: Put the steamed edamame pods in a large bowl. Add the seasoning mix to the edamame and gently toss to coat everything.
4. Change the seasoning: Check the seasonings and make any changes you want. You can add more soy sauce, rice vinegar, sesame oil, or red pepper flakes to make the dish taste saucier, saltier, or tangier.
5. Serve right away: As a healthy snack or side dish, the spicy Asian edamame pods are great.

FISH & SEAFOOD

61. NEW ENGLAND-STYLE STEAMED LOBSTER TAILS

Prep Time: 10 minutes | Cook Time: 8-12 minutes

Total Time: 20-23 minutes | Servings: 2

Ingredients

- 1/2 tbsp lemon juice
- 2 live or thawed lobster tails (1-1.5 pounds each)
- 2-3 tbsp melted butter
- 1/4 tsp Old Bay seasoning (optional)
- 1/4 tsp dried tarragon (optional)
- Freshly cracked black pepper, to taste
- Fresh lemon wedges, for serving

Instructions

1. Get the lobster tails ready. If you're using live lobsters, kill them humanely according to good manners. If you need to, thaw frozen lobster tails. Cut the top shell lengthwise with kitchen shears, stopping just before the tail splits in half. Take out the meat with care, leaving the vein attached to the shell. Run cold water over the meat and vein.
2. Get the steamer ready: Follow the directions on the package to add one to two inches of water to your electric steamer. Heat the water.
3. Spice up the lobster: Cream the butter and add the lemon juice, tarragon (if you want to use it), Old Bay seasoning (if you want to use it), and black pepper. Spread a lot of the seasoning mix over the lobster meat.
4. Put the lobster tails in the steamer basket with the vein side facing up to steam the lobster. For 1- to 1.25-pound tails, cover and steam for 8- 10 minutes. For 1.25- to 1.5-pound tails, steam for 10- 12 minutes. Do not look! If you cook the meat too long, it will get tough.
5. To see if it's done, gently stick a skewer into the thickest part of the tail after steaming it. If the meat is clear and slides right in, it's done.
6. Serve right away: Move the lobster tails carefully to the plates. An egg cracker or nutcracker can be used to open the shells. Serve with lemon wedges, melted butter, and your favorite dipping sauce, like a cocktail or drawn butter.

62. SPICY CAJUN SHRIMP BOIL

Prep Time: 10 minutes | Cook Time: 15 minutes

Total Time: 25 minutes | Servings: 4

Ingredients

- 1 pound corn on the cob, broken in half
- 2 cloves garlic, minced
- 1 pound small potatoes, halved
- 1 red bell pepper, diced
- 1/4 tsp black pepper
- 1 cup of water
- 1 (12-ounce) bottle beer
- 1 tbsp olive oil
- 1/2 tsp Cajun seasoning
- 1 green bell pepper, diced
- 1 pound large shrimp, peeled and deveined
- 1 celery stalk, diced
- 1/2 onion, diced
- 1/4 tsp cayenne pepper (optional)
- Fresh lemon wedges, for serving

Instructions

1. Following the directions on the package ad,d one to two inches of water to your electric steamer.
2. Spice up the shrimp in a large bowl with cayenne pepper, black pepper, olive oil, and Cajun seasoning.
3. The bell peppers, celery, onion, and garlic should all be put in the steamer basket. Add pepper and salt.
4. Arrange the shrimp on top of the other foods.
5. Put the water and beer into the steamer pot.
6. Cover and put the steamer basket on top.
7. It needs to be steamed for 15 minutes or until the shrimp are pink and opaque and the vegetables are soft.
8. Put the corn and potatoes in the steamer basket. Steam for another 5 minutes or until the potatoes are soft.
9. Serve right away with lemon wedges.

63. STEAMED SCALLOPS WITH LEMON BUTTER SAUCE

Prep Time: 5 minutes | Cook Time: 8-10 minutes

Total Time: 13-15 minutes | Servings: 2

Ingredients

- 12 sea scallops, dry or wet
- 1 tbsp olive oil
- 1 tbsp unsalted butter
- 2 tbsp freshly squeezed lemon juice
- Salt and freshly cracked black pepper, to taste
- 1/4 cup of dry white wine or chicken broth
- 1/4 tsp chopped fresh parsley, for garnish (optional)

Instructions

1. Get the scallops ready: There is no difference between "dry" and "wet" scallops when toweling them down.
2. Spice up the scallops: Add a little salt and pepper to each scallop.
3. Warm up the scallops: Follow the directions on the package to fill your electric steamer with water and bring it to a slow boil. Place the scallops in the steamer basket so that they are all in one layer—steam for 4 to 5 minutes for large scallops or 3 to 4 minutes for small scallops. If you cook them too long, they will get tough.
4. First, steam the scallops. Then, melt the butter in a small saucepan over medium-low heat. Then put the lemon juice and white wine or broth. Slowly cook until the liquid is almost gone, for about two to three minutes. Add pepper and salt to taste.
5. To serve, carefully move the scallops from the steamer to the plates. Add the hot lemon butter sauce to the scallops and, if you want, top them with chopped parsley.

64. ASIAN-STYLE STEAMED FISH IN BANANA LEAVES

Prep Time: 15 minutes | Cook Time: 15-20 minutes

Total Time: 30-35 minutes | Servings: 2

Ingredients

- 1 tbsp rice vinegar
- 1 tbsp minced ginger
- 1 scallion, thinly sliced (optional)
- 1 whole fish (around 1 pound), cleaned and scaled (white fish like cod or snapper works well)
- 1 clove garlic, minced
- 2 large banana leaves, softened by heating over a flame or in hot water for 30 seconds
- 1/2 red bell pepper, thinly sliced (optional)
- 1 tbsp oyster sauce (optional)
- 1 tbsp sesame oil
- 1 tbsp soy sauce
- Salt and freshly cracked black pepper, to taste
- Cilantro sprigs, for garnish (optional)

Instructions

1. Get the fish ready: You can dry the fish on paper towels and make shallow cuts on both sides of it if you want to.
2. Season the fish: Put soy sauce, oyster sauce (if you're using it), rice vinegar, sesame oil, ginger, and garlic in a small bowl. Put the marinade on the fish and inside the cavity and rub it in. Wait ten minutes.
3. Get the banana leaves ready: Put one banana leaf flat on the ground so the shiny side faces down. Put the fish in the middle. When you're done cooking the fish, put the red bell pepper and scallion slices on top of it. Roll the leaf up around the fish and fold the sides over it. Then, roll the bottom end up. To make a sealed packet, fold the top end down. To make a double layer, do it again with the second banana leaf.
4. To steam the fish, follow the directions on the package and fill your electric steamer with water. Then, bring it to a boil. Cover the fish in banana leaves and put it in the steamer basket. Steam for 15 to 20 minutes or until the fish is opaque and cooked all the way through. To find out if the fish is done, stick a fork into the thickest part of it. It should be easy to flake.
5. To serve, carefully move the banana leaf packet to a plate. Carefully open the package to find the fish inside. If you want, you can add cilantro sprigs as a garnish. Serve with steamed rice or vegetables.

65. STEAMED LEMONGRASS SALMON WITH COCONUT RICE

Prep Time: 15 minutes | Cook Time: 20 minutes

Total Time: 35 minutes | Servings: 2

Ingredients

For the Lemongrass Salmon:

- 1/4 tsp garlic powder
- 2 salmon fillets (6-8 ounce each)
- 1 tbsp soy sauce
- 2 stalks lemongrass, white part only, thinly sliced
- 1 tbsp olive oil
- 1/2 tsp grated ginger
- Salt and pepper to taste

For the Coconut Rice:

- 1 1/2 cups of coconut milk
- 1/2 cup of water
- 1/4 tsp salt
- 1 cup of jasmine rice, rinsed
- 1 pandan leaf (optional)

Instructions

1. Mix the almond milk, garlic powder, ginger, olive oil, salt, and pepper in a tiny dish. This is how you make the lemongrass salmon.
2. Wet the salmon fillets with paper towels and pat them dry. Put them in a baking dish or steamer basket that is big enough to hold them side by side.
3. Put the lemongrass slices on top of the salmon fillets. Cover the salmon and lemongrass with the soy sauce mixture by pouring it over them
4. Prepare the coconut rice: Rinse the jasmine rice and put it in the pot with coconut milk, water, and salt. If you want to, add the pandan leaf.
5. We steam together: Follow the directions on the package to fill your electric steamer with water and then bring it to a boil. On top of the pot with the coconut rice, put the steamer basket with the salmon. The rice should be soft and fluffy, and the salmon should be cooked through. Cover and steam for 20 minutes.
6. Put out: Move the salmon fillets carefully to plates. Use a fork to fluff the rice, then serve it with the salmon. Add more fresh lemongrass or cilantro as a garnish if you want.

66. HAWAIIAN STEAMED MAHI MAHI WITH MANGO SALSA

Prep Time: 15 minutes | Cook Time: 10-12 minutes

Total Time: 25-27 minutes | Servings: 2

Ingredients

For the Mahi Mahi:

- 1 tbsp soy sauce
- 2 mahi mahi fillets (6-8 ounce each)
- 1/4 tsp garlic powder
- 1 tbsp lime juice
- 1/2 tsp minced ginger
- Salt and pepper to taste

For the Mango Salsa:

- 1/4 red onion, thinly sliced
- 1 ripe mango, peeled, pitted, and diced
- 1 tbsp chopped fresh cilantro
- 1/2 red bell pepper, seeded and diced
- 1/2 tsp olive oil
- 1 tbsp lime juice
- 1 Jalapeno pepper, seeded and minced (optional)
- Salt and pepper to taste

Instructions

1. Prepare the marinade: Melt the garlic powder, ginger, salt, and pepper in a tiny bowl. Add the lime juice and whisk them together.
2. Season the mahi mahi with: You can use paper towels to dry the mahi mahi fillets. Put them in a baking dish or steamer basket that is big enough to hold them side by side.
3. Cover the mahi mahi with the marinade by pouring it over them. Leave them to sit for at least 10 minutes or up to 30 minutes if you want a stronger flavor.
4. How to make the mango salsa: Put the diced mango, red bell pepper, red onion, Jalapeno (if using), cilantro, lime juice, olive oil, salt, and pepper in a bowl. Let this sit while you prepare the mahi mahi. After mixing well, set it aside.
5. Mahi Mahi should be steamed: Follow the directions on the package to fill your electric steamer with water and then bring it to a boil. Put the mahi mahi in the steamer basket on top of the pot. Put the lid on top and steam for 10 to 12 minutes, or until the mahi mahi is opaque and cooked through.
6. Put out: Move the cooked mahi mahi fillets carefully to plates. Add the cool mango salsa on top, and enjoy!

67. STEAMED TILAPIA WITH TROPICAL FRUIT SALSA

Prep Time: 10 minutes | Cook Time: 8-10 minutes

Total Time: 20-22 minutes | Servings: 2

Ingredients

For the Tilapia:

- 1/2 tsp dried thyme
- 1 tbsp olive oil
- 2 tilapia fillets (6-8 ounce each)
- Salt and pepper to taste

For the Tropical Fruit Salsa:

- 1 ripe mango, peeled, pitted, and diced
- 1 Jalapeno pepper, seeded and minced (optional)
- 1/2 pineapple, peeled, cored, and diced
- 1/4 red bell pepper, seeded and diced
- 1 tbsp chopped fresh cilantro
- 1 tbsp lime juice
- 1/2 tsp honey
- 1/4 red onion, thinly sliced
- Salt and pepper to taste

Instructions

1. To prepare the tilapia, follow the manufacturer's instructions and heat your electric steamer.
2. You can use tissue paper to dry the tilapia fillets. Stack them one on top of the other in a steamer basket.
3. Add thyme, salt, and pepper to the tilapia after brushing it with olive oil.
4. Get the salsa ready: In a bowl, mix the diced mango, pineapple, red bell pepper, red onion, Jalapeno (if using), cilantro, lime juice, honey, salt, and pepper while the steamer heats up. After mixing well, set it aside.
5. Put the basket with the fish inside the hot steamer to steam the tilapia and cover it. The tilapia should be steamed for 8 to 10 minutes or until it is opaque and cooked.
6. Put out: Move the cooked tilapia fillets carefully to the plates. Add the excellent tropical fruit salsa on top, and enjoy!

68. STEAMED CLAMS WITH CHORIZO AND WHITE WINE

Prep Time: 5 minutes | Cook Time: 10 minutes

Total Time: 15 minutes | Servings: 2

Ingredients

- 2 cloves garlic, minced
- 1/4 cup of chopped fresh parsley
- 1 tbsp olive oil
- 1/2 cup of dry white wine
- 1/2 onion, diced
- 1/2 link Spanish chorizo, diced
- 2 pounds littleneck clams, scrubbed and rinsed
- 1/4 tsp red pepper flakes (optional)
- Salt and freshly cracked black pepper, to taste
- Crusty bread, for serving (optional)

Instructions

1. Get the steamer ready: Follow the directions on the package to fill your electric steamer with water and bring it to a slow boil.
2. Warm up the oil and cook: In a big pan over medium-low heat, warm the olive oil. After you add the onion, cook for about 3 minutes or until it gets soft. Add the chorizo and garlic and stir them in. Cook for one more minute.
3. White wine is used to deglaze. It is poured into the pan and scrapes up any browned bits. Bring it to a slow boil and cook for two minutes to remove the alcohol.
4. Put the clams in the pan with the wine mixture to steam them. Put the lid on top and steam for 5 to 7 minutes or until the clams open. Delete any clams that aren't opened.
5. Finish up and serve: Add the red pepper flakes and parsley; if you want, season with salt and pepper. Put the clams and broth in bowls or a big pot for serving. Serve right away with crusty bread to dip (not required).

69. CANTONESE STEAMED FISH WITH SOY SAUCE AND GINGER

Prep Time: 10 minutes | Cook Time: 8-12 minutes

Total Time: 20-23 minutes | Servings: 2

Ingredients

- 1 inch ginger, thinly julienned
- 2 tbsp light soy sauce
- 1 tbsp vegetable oil
- 1 tbsp chopped scallions
- 1 whole fish (1-1.5 pounds), cleaned and scaled (white fish like sea bass, grouper, or snapper work well)
- 1/2 tsp sesame oil (optional)
- 1 tbsp Shaoxing wine (optional)
- Cilantro sprigs, for garnish (optional)

Instructions

1. Get the fish ready: You can speed up and even out the cooking of the fish by cutting it diagonally on both sides. For drying the fish, you can use a paper towel.
2. Season the fish: Soy sauce, Shaoxing wine (if using), and 1 tbsp of vegetable oil should all be mixed in a small bowl. Spread the sauce all over the fish, inside and out. Wait ten minutes.
3. Get the steamer ready: Follow the directions on the package to fill your electric steamer with water and bring it to a slow boil.
4. Cook the fish: Put the fish on a plate or other heat-safe dish that can fit in the steamer basket. Put the ginger and scallions on top of the fish. Cover the dish and put it in the steamer basket. Steam the fish for 8 to 12 minutes or until it's opaque and cooked. To find out if the fish is done, stick a fork into the thickest part of it. It should be easy to flake.
5. In a small pan, heat the last tbsp of vegetable oil until it starts to smoke. Pour the hot oil over the fish that has been steamed.
6. Serve: Carefully move the fish from the steamer to a plate for serving. If you want, you can add cilantro sprigs as a garnish. Serve with steamed rice and vegetables.

70. VIETNAMESE STEAMED FISH WITH NUOC CHAM SAUCE

Prep Time: 15 minutes | Cook Time: 8-10 minutes

Total Time: 23-25 minutes | Servings: 2

Ingredients

For the Fish:

- 1/2 tsp minced ginger
- 1 tbsp lime juice
- 1/4 tsp garlic powder
- 1 whole fish (1-1.5 pounds), cleaned and scaled
- 1 tbsp sugar
- 2 tbsp fish sauce
- Salt and freshly cracked black pepper, to taste
- Banana leaves (optional)

For the Nuoc Cham Sauce:

- 1/4 cup of fish sauce
- 1 small carrot, julienned
- 1/4 cup of water
- 1 tbsp sugar
- 1 small red chili pepper, (optional)
- 1/4 cup of lime juice
- 1 clove garlic, thinly sliced
- Fresh cilantro sprigs, for garnish

Instructions

1. Get the fish ready. If you want to cook it faster and more evenly, make shallow diagonal cuts on both sides of the fish. For drying the fish, you can use a paper towel.
2. Season the fish: Put sugar, ginger, garlic powder, salt, and pepper in a small bowl. Add the fish sauce and mix them. Spread the sauce all over the fish, inside and out. Wait ten minutes.
3. Get the steamer ready: Follow the directions on the package to fill your electric steamer with water and bring it to a slow boil.
4. If you want to, prepare the banana leaves: Put one banana leaf flat, shiny side down if you're going to use it. Put the fish in the middle. Roll the leaf up around the fish and fold the sides over it. Then, roll the bottom end up. To make a sealed packet, fold the top end down. To make a double layer, do it again with the second banana leaf.
5. To steam the fish, put it on a plate or pot that can handle heat that fits in the steamer basket. You can put the fish in the banana leaf packet or not. Cover the dish and put it in the steamer basket. The fish should be steamed for 8 to 10 minutes or until it is opaque and cooked. To find out if the fish is done, stick a fork into the thickest part of it. It should be easy to flake.
6. Get the nuoc cham sauce ready. Mix the fish sauce, water, lime juice, and sugar in a tiny bowl with a whisk while the fish steams. Slice the carrot and add it with the garlic and chili pepper if used. Leave it for five minutes or more to let the flavors fill in.
7. Put out: Move the steamed fish carefully to a plate for serving. Serve with the nuoc cham sauce for dipping and fresh cilantro sprigs on top.

71. STEAMED MUSSELS WITH GARLIC WHITE WINE BROTH

Prep Time: 5 minutes | Cook Time: 10-12 minutes

Total Time: 15-17 minutes | Servings: 2-3

Ingredients

- 2 pounds mussels, debearded and rinsed
- 1 tbsp olive oil
- 1 shallot, minced
- 2 cloves garlic, minced
- 1/2 cup of dry white wine
- 1/2 cup of chicken broth or water
- 1/4 cup of chopped fresh parsley
- Salt and freshly cracked black pepper, to taste
- Crusty bread, for serving (optional)

Instructions

1. Get the steamer ready: Follow the directions on the package to fill your electric steamer with water and bring it to a slow boil.
2. Warm up the oil and cook: In a large pan, heat olive oil over medium-low heat. After you add the shallot, cook it for about 3 minutes until it gets soft. Put the garlic and cook for one more minute, watching out not to burn.
3. Add wine and broth to deglaze: White wine and chicken broth (or water) should be added. Scrub the bottom of the pan to get rid of any browned bits. Bring it to a slow boil and cook for two minutes to get rid of the alcohol.
4. To steam the mussels, put them in a pan with wine and water. Cover and steam for 5-7 minutes, or until the mussels open up all the way. Don't eat any mussels that aren't open.
5. The finishing touches: Add the parsley and season with salt and pepper to taste. Move the broth and mussels to bowls for serving or a big pot.
6. Serve: Serve right away with crusty bread to dip (optional). Enjoy the tasty broth and soft mussels!

72. THAI STEAMED FISH CAKES WITH SWEET CHILI SAUCE

Prep Time: 15 minutes | Cook Time: 12-15 minutes

Total Time: 27-30 minutes | Servings: 2-3

Ingredients

For the Fish Cakes:

- 1 tbsp fish sauce
- 12 ounce skinless white fish fillets (cod, haddock, or tilapia work well)
- 2 tbsp chopped red onion
- 1 tbsp grated ginger
- 1/4 cup of chopped fresh cilantro
- 1 egg, beaten
- 1/4 cup of chopped red bell pepper
- 1 tbsp lime juice
- 1/2 cup of chopped green beans
- 1 tbsp cornstarch
- 1 clove garlic, minced
- Salt and freshly cracked black pepper to taste

For the Sweet Chili Sauce (Optional):

- 1/4 cup of rice vinegar
- 1 tbsp lime juice
- 1/2 tsp minced ginger
- 1/4 cup of red chili sauce
- 1 tbsp sugar
- 1/4 tsp minced garlic
- Pinch of red pepper flakes (optional)

Instructions

1. To make the fish cakes, cut the fish fillets into small pieces. Make small pieces of the fish, bell pepper, cilantro, green beans, and red onion in a food processor. Make sure the food is not mushy.
2. Put it in a bowl and add the cornstarch, fish sauce, lime juice, ginger, garlic, egg, and ginger. Add pepper and salt to taste. Mix well until everything is well mixed.
3. Make small patties out of the mixture about 2 to 3 inches across.
4. Get the steamer ready: Follow the directions on the package to fill your electric steamer with water and bring it to a slow boil.
5. Put the fish cakes in the steamer: Stack the fish cakes one on top of the other on a plate or basket that fits in your steamer. Place the lid on top and steam for 12-15 minutes or until the food is fully cooked and the color is clear.
6. While the fish cakes are cooking, make the sweet chili sauce. Mix red chili sauce, garlic, rice vinegar, sugar, lime juice, ginger, and red pepper flakes (if using) in a small bowl with a whisk.
7. To serve, carefully move the fish cakes from the steamer to the plates. You can drizzle the dish with sweet chili sauce and top it off with fresh cilantro sprigs. I like to serve it with vegetables or steamed rice.

POULTRY

73. SPICY GARLIC GINGER CHICKEN

Prep Time: 15 minutes | Cook Time: 15-20 minutes

Total Time: 30-35 minutes | Servings: 2

Ingredients

- 1 tbsp sesame oil
- 1 tbsp honey
- 2 tbsp soy sauce
- 1 tbsp rice vinegar
- 1/2 tsp cornstarch
- 1 red chili pepper, thinly sliced (adjust to your desired spice level)
- 2 tbsp chopped green onions
- 1 tbsp minced ginger
- 2 cloves garlic, minced
- 1 pound boneless, skinless chicken breasts or thighs, cut into bite-sized pieces

Instructions

1. Soy sauce, sesame oil, chili pepper, honey, rice vinegar, ginger, garlic, and cornstarch should all be mixed in a bowl. This is the marinade.
2. Make the chicken marinade: Put the chicken pieces in it and toss them to cover them. Let it sit for at least 15 or 30 minutes if you want it to taste even better.
3. Get the steamer ready: Follow the directions on the package to fill your electric steamer with water and then bring it to a boil.
4. Steam the chicken: Marinated chicken pieces in a steamer basket so they are all packed together. Put the lid on top and steam for 15 to 20 minutes or until the chicken is opaque and cooked through. Insert a fork into the thickest part of the chicken to see if it's done. It should be easy to flake.
5. Add the chopped green onions to the chicken while it's still steaming.
6. To serve, carefully move the chicken from the steamer to the plates. Serve the tasty and healthy dish with steamed rice or vegetables, and enjoy!

74. ASIAN-STYLE CHICKEN LETTUCE WRAPS

Prep Time: 15 minutes | Cook Time: 10-12 minutes

Total Time: 25-27 minutes | Servings: 2-3

Ingredients

For the Chicken Filling:

- 1 tbsp sesame oil
- 1 tsp minced ginger
- 1 clove garlic, minced
- 1/2 tsp red pepper flakes
- 1 tbsp rice vinegar
- 1/4 cup of chopped green onions
- 1 pound ground chicken
- 1 tbsp brown sugar
- 1 tbsp oyster sauce (optional)
- 1/4 tsp ground black pepper
- 2 tbsp soy sauce

For the Lettuce Wraps:

- 1 head romaine lettuce, leaves separated and washed
- 1 head butter lettuce (optional), leaves separated and washed

For the Toppings (optional):

- Hoisin sauce
- Bean sprouts
- Sriracha mayo
- Fresh herbs like cilantro and mint
- Peanut sauce
- Sliced bell peppers
- Chopped cucumber
- Shredded carrots

Instructions

1. Put the soy sauce, oyster sauce (if using), sesame oil, brown sugar, ginger, rice vinegar, garlic, red pepper flakes, and black pepper. Mix the ingredients using a whisk.
2. Let the chicken soak in the sauce. Add the ground chicken to the sauce and mix it well to cover it evenly. It should be marinated for at least 15 minutes, but up to 30 minutes will strengthen the flavor.
3. Get the steamer ready: Follow the directions on the package to fill your electric steamer with water and then bring it to a boil.
4. Put the chicken marinated in a single layer in a steamer basket. Put the lid on top and steam for 10 to 12 minutes or until the chicken is opaque and cooked through. Use a fork to break up the chicken while it's cooking.
5. You can make the toppings while the chicken is cooking: Cut or shred the desired herbs and vegetables. Get any sauces you want to use ready.
6. Put the lettuce wraps together by arranging each person's leaves on a platter or plate. Put some steamed chicken and the toppings of your choice in each leaf. Add your favorite sauce (not required).
7. Serve: Enjoy your tasty and healthy chicken lettuce wraps made in an Asian style!

75. CHICKEN AND VEGETABLE SKEWERS

Prep Time: 15 minutes | Cook Time: 12-15 minutes

Total Time: 27-30 minutes | Servings: 2-3

Ingredients

- 8-10 wooden skewers, soaked in water for at least 30 minutes (optional)
- 1 tbsp honey
- 1 pound boneless, skinless chicken breasts or thighs, cut into bite-sized pieces
- 1 tbsp rice vinegar
- 1 zucchini, cut into chunks
- 1 clove garlic, minced
- 1/2 tsp ground black pepper
- 1/2 yellow bell pepper, cut into chunks
- 1 small onion, cut into wedges
- 1 tbsp olive oil
- 1/2 green bell pepper, cut into chunks
- 1 tsp minced ginger
- 1/2 red bell pepper, cut into chunks
- 1 tbsp soy sauce
- Salt to taste

Instructions

1. Prepare the marinade: Mix soy sauce, rice vinegar, garlic, ginger, honey, and black pepper in a bowl with a whisk.
2. Make the chicken and vegetables marinate: Add the vegetables and chicken pieces to the marinade and toss to coat everything. It should be marinated for at least 15 minutes, but up to 30 minutes will strengthen the flavor.
3. Get the steamer ready: Follow the directions on the package to fill your electric steamer with water and then bring it to a boil.
4. Put the skewers together: Put the chicken and vegetables on the wet wooden skewers in a pattern that goes from left to right. Metal skewers that don't need to be soaked can also be used.
5. Make the skewers steamy: Stack the skewers one on top of the other in a steamer basket. Put the lid on top and steam for 12-15 minutes until the vegetables are soft but still crisp and the chicken is cooked through. Insert a fork into the thickest part of the chicken to see if it's done. It should be easy to flake.
6. While the skewers are cooking, you can (optionally) prepare your serving dish. You can make a bed of cooked rice or quinoa to put the skewers on.
7. Serve: Carefully move the skewers from the steamer to plates or a serving dish. Enjoy right away!

76. STEAMED CHICKEN AND DUMPLINGS

Prep Time: 20 minutes | Cook Time: 15-20 minutes | Total Time: 35-40 minutes | Servings: 4

Ingredients

For the Chicken:

- 1 tbsp cornstarch
- 1/4 tsp ground ginger
- 1 tbsp soy sauce
- 1 pound boneless
- 1 clove garlic, minced
- 1/2 tsp sesame oil
- 1 tbsp Shaoxing wine (optional)
- Salt and freshly cracked black pepper to taste

For the Dumplings:

- 1/4 cup of chopped cabbage or napa cabbage
- 1 tsp sesame oil
- 20 wonton wrappers
- 1/2 tsp minced ginger
- 1/4 cup of chopped scallions
- 1/2 pound ground pork or chicken
- 1 clove garlic, minced
- 1 tbsp soy sauce
- 1 tbsp oyster sauce (optional)
- Salt and freshly cracked black pepper to taste

For the Sauce (optional):

- 1 tsp chopped scallions
- 1 tbsp sesame oil
- 1 tbsp soy sauce
- 1 tbsp rice vinegar

Instructions

1. To marinate the chicken, put soy sauce, cornstarch, sesame oil, garlic, salt, ginger, and pepper in a bowl. If you want to use Shaoxing wine, add it now. Cover the chicken pieces with the sauce by tossing them in it. Let it sit for at least 15 or 30 minutes if you want it to taste even better.
2. Prepare the dumplings: Soy sauce, oyster sauce (if using), sesame oil, ginger, garlic, salt, and pepper should all be mixed in a different bowl with the ground meat.
3. Put the dumplings inside and fold them over. Spread a large filling in the middle of each wonton wrapper. Wet the edges with water, then fold them over to make the shape of a crescent moon. Pinch the edges together to seal them. Do it again with the rest of the wrappers and filling.
4. Follow the directions on the package to fill your electric steamer with water and bring it to a slow boil.
5. Put the chicken pieces on a plate in your steamer basket so they are all in one layer. Then, steam the chicken and dumplings. Put the dumplings on a separate plate or steamer liner (this will make them easier to take out). Place the plate of dumplings on top of the plate of chicken. Place the lid on top and steam for 15 to 20 minutes until the chicken is done and the dumplings are clear and cooked.

6. While the chicken and dumplings are cooking, make the sauce, if you want to: And chop scallions. In a small dish, mix sesame oil, soy sauce, and rice vinegar together.
7. To serve, carefully move the chicken and dumplings to plates. Add the sauce if you want to and enjoy!

77. STEAMED CHICKEN AND CORNBREAD STUFFING

Prep Time: 20 minutes | Cook Time: 20-25 minutes | Total Time: 40-45 minutes | Servings: 4

Ingredients

For the Chicken:

- 1 whole chicken (3-4 pounds), cleaned and seasoned with salt and pepper

For the Cornbread Stuffing:

- 1/4 cup of diced onion
- 1/2 cup of chicken broth
- 1 tbsp melted butter
- 2 tbsp chopped fresh parsley
- 1/2 cup of diced celery
- 2 cups of crumbled cornbread
- 1/4 tsp poultry seasoning
- 1/2 tsp dried thyme
- 1/4 cup of dried cranberries (optional)
- 1/4 cup of chopped walnuts (optional)
- Salt and freshly cracked black pepper to taste

Instructions

1. Get the chicken ready. Season the chicken all over, inside and out, with salt and pepper.
2. Crumbled cornbread, celery, onion, parsley, melted butter, chicken broth, walnuts (if using), cranberries (if using), thyme, poultry seasoning, salt, and pepper should all be mixed together in a large bowl. Combine well by mixing.
3. Fill the chicken: Spread the cornbread stuffing mixture out in a loose layer inside the chicken. You can use kitchen twine or toothpicks to close the hole if you want to.
4. Get the steamer ready: Follow the directions on the package to fill your electric steamer with water and bring it to a slow boil.
5. Stuff the chicken and put it in the steamer basket. Place the chicken on a plate or steamer rack that fits in the steamer basket. It's done when the chicken is cooked through and the juices run clear when you stick a fork into the thickest part of the thigh. Cover and steam for 20-25 minutes. The chicken should be cooked all the way through to 165°F. Rest the chicken: After cooking, put the chicken on a plate and wait 10 minutes before cutting it up.
6. Serve: Cut the chicken into pieces and put them on a plate with the cornbread stuffing. Enjoy!

78. HONEY MUSTARD GLAZED CHICKEN DRUMSTICKS

Prep Time: 15 minutes | Cook Time: 20-25 minutes

Total Time: 35-40 minutes | Servings: 4

Ingredients

- 1 tbsp soy sauce
- 1/2 tsp garlic powder
- 1 tbsp brown sugar
- 1 tbsp olive oil
- 1/4 tsp black pepper
- 1 tbsp Dijon mustard
- 8 chicken drumsticks
- 2 tbsp honey
- 1/4 tsp paprika (optional)
- Fresh parsley, for garnish (optional)

Instructions

1. Warm up the steamer: Follow the directions on the package to fill your electric steamer with water and bring it to a slow boil.
2. Dry off the drumsticks: Use paper towels to soak up any extra water to dry the chicken drumsticks.
3. How to make the glaze: Mix honey, soy sauce, brown sugar, garlic powder, black pepper, paprika (if using), and olive oil in a tiny bowl with a whisk.
4. Wrap the drumsticks in. Spread a lot of glaze over each drumstick with a brush or a spoon, ensuring all sides are covered.
5. Place the glazed drumsticks in a single layer in the steamer basket. This will help the drumsticks cook. There should be a top lid. Steam for 20 to 25 minutes until the chicken is done and the temperature inside reaches 165°F. A meat thermometer can be put into the thickest part of the thigh to see if it's done.
6. Broil for extra glaze (optional): Preheat your oven's broiler to high if you want the skin to be crispier and the glaze to taste more robust. Move the steamed drumsticks carefully to a baking sheet lined with foil. Watch it closely while you broil for 3 to 5 minutes or until the glaze bubbles and turns a little caramelized.
7. Add the toppings and serve. Put the cooked drumsticks on a plate for serving. You can sprinkle fresh parsley on top if you like. Put it out immediately and dip it in blue cheese, ranch dressing, or any other sauce you like.

79. STEAMED CHICKEN AND VEGETABLE MEDLEY

Prep Time: 15 minutes | Cook Time: 15-20 minutes | Total Time: 30-35 minutes | Servings: 4

Ingredients

For the Chicken:

- 1/4 tsp garlic powder
- 1/2 tsp ginger powder
- 1 pound boneless
- 1 tbsp soy sauce
- 1 tbsp sesame oil
- 1 tbsp rice vinegar
- Salt and freshly cracked black pepper to taste

For the Vegetable Medley:

- 1/4 cup of chopped green onions
- 1/2 tsp dried thyme
- 1/4 tsp salt
- 1 cup of sliced bell peppers
- 1/4 tsp freshly cracked black pepper
- 1 cup of broccoli florets
- 1/2 cup of sugar snap peas
- 1 tbsp olive oil
- 1 cup of baby carrots

For the Sauce (optional):

- 1 tbsp rice vinegar
- 1/2 tsp honey
- 1 tsp sriracha (optional)
- 2 tbsp soy sauce
- 1 tbsp sesame oil

Instructions

1. To prepare the chicken, mix soy sauce, rice vinegar, sesame oil, ginger powder, garlic powder, salt, and pepper in a bowl. Cover the chicken pieces with the sauce by tossing them in it. Let it sit for at least 15 or 30 minutes if you want it to taste even better.
2. Get the steamer ready: Follow the directions on the package to fill your electric steamer with water and bring it to a slow boil.
3. Put the steamer together: Outline the chicken pieces marinated on a plate or steamer rack that can fit inside your basket. Put the broccoli florets on a separate plate or a steamer liner and put it on top of the chicken. This will help them steam faster. You can also put different vegetables on different trays or plates based on how long they need to cook.
4. Put the chicken and vegetables in a steamer. Put the lid on top and steam for 15 to 20 minutes until the chicken is done and the vegetables are soft but still crisp. Insert a fork into the thickest part of the chicken to see if it's done. It should be easy to flake.
5. As the chicken and vegetables steam, you can make the sauce if you want to. Put soy sauce, rice vinegar, sesame oil, sriracha (if using), and honey in a small bowl. Mix them with a whisk.
6. To serve, carefully move the cooked chicken and vegetables to plates. Add the sauce to the dish and then sprinkle chopped green onions on top. Enjoy yourself!

80. HERB-CRUSTED STEAMED CHICKEN BREASTS

Prep Time: 10 minutes | Cook Time: 15-20 minutes

Total Time: 25-30 minutes | Servings: 2

Ingredients

- 1/4 tsp dried oregano
- 1 tbsp olive oil
- 1/2 tsp dried thyme
- 1/2 tsp dried rosemary
- 1/4 tsp garlic powder
- 2 boneless, skinless chicken breasts (6-8 ounce each)
- Salt and freshly cracked black pepper to taste
- Optional: 1/4 tsp red pepper flakes (for a spicy kick)

Instructions

1. Warm up the steamer: Follow the directions on the package to fill your electric steamer with water and bring it to a slow boil.
2. Get the herb crust ready: Add the garlic powder, salt, rosemary, pepper, red pepper flakes (if using), thyme, oregano, and olive oil, and mix them all together in a small bowl. Mix the herbs together well to make a fragrant mix.
3. Cover the chicken: Use paper towels to dry the chicken breasts. Make sure that all sides of each chicken breast are covered by the herb mixture that you rub on them.
4. Cook the chicken in water: You should put the chicken breasts that have been covered in herbs in a single layer in the steamer basket. Keep the lid on and steam for 15 to 20 minutes, or until the chicken is done and the temperature inside reaches 165°F. A meat thermometer can be put into the thickest part of the chicken to see if it's done.
5. Take a break and serve: After the chicken breasts are done, put them on a plate and let them rest for a few minutes. This lets the juices move around, which makes the meat more tender and flavorful.
6. Have fun! You can serve the chicken breasts sliced up with your favorite sides, like rice, roasted potatoes, or steamed vegetables. To make them taste even better, you can put and drizzle them with more olive oil, lemon juice, or your favorite sauce.

81. LEMON GARLIC CHICKEN WINGS

Prep Time: 15 minutes | Cook Time: 20-25 minutes

Total Time: 35-40 minutes | Servings: 2-3

Ingredients

- 1/4 tsp freshly cracked black pepper
- 1 tbsp lemon juice
- 2 cloves garlic, minced
- 1/4 tsp salt
- 1/2 tsp dried oregano
- 1 tbsp olive oil
- 1 pound chicken wings (about 8-10 wings)
- Optional: Pinch of red pepper flakes

Instructions

1. Get the steamer ready: Follow the directions on the package to fill your electric steamer with water and bring it to a slow boil.
2. Dry the chicken wings with paper towels: Take off any extra feathers on the wings and use paper towels to dry them.
3. Prepare the sauce: Using a whisk, mix the garlic, oregano, salt, pepper, red pepper flakes (if using), olive oil, and lemon juice in a bowl.
4. Season the wings: Toss the chicken wings in the marinade, making sure that each one gets a good coat. Let it sit for at least 15 minutes or up to 30 minutes if you want it to taste even better.
5. Put the chicken wings that have been marinated in a single layer in the basket of your steamer. There should be a lid on top. Steam for 20 to 25 minutes until the chicken is done and the temperature inside reaches 165°F. A meat thermometer can be put into the thickest part of a wing to see if it's done.
6. For extra crispiness, you can boil it. Preheat your oven's broiler to high. Move the steamed wings carefully to a baking sheet that has been lined with foil. Watch closely while broiling for three to five minutes or until the skin is golden brown and crispy.
7. Serve the chicken wings by putting them on a plate. Add fresh parsley or lemon wedges as a garnish to make it look nice and taste better. You can dip them in buffalo sauce, ranch dressing, blue cheese dressing, or any other sauce you like.

82. CHICKEN AND QUINOA STUFFED PEPPERS

Prep Time: 20 minutes | Cook Time: 40-45 minutes

Total Time: 60-65 minutes | Servings: 4

Ingredients

For the Peppers:

- 4 bell peppers (red, yellow, orange, or a mix)
- 1 tbsp olive oil
- Salt and freshly cracked black pepper to taste

For the Chicken and Quinoa Stuffing:

- 1 tbsp tomato paste
- 1/4 cup of diced celery
- 1 pound ground chicken
- 1/4 cup of chopped fresh parsley
- 1 cup of cooked quinoa
- 2 cloves garlic, minced
- 1/2 cup of diced tomatoes (fresh or canned)
- 1/2 cup of diced onion
- 1/4 tsp chili powder
- 1/2 tsp ground cumin
- 1 tsp dried oregano
- Salt and freshly cracked black pepper to taste

For the Sauce (optional):

- 1/2 tsp dried oregano
- 1 cup of crushed tomatoes (canned)
- 1 tbsp tomato paste
- 1 tsp brown sugar
- 1/2 cup of chicken broth
- Salt and freshly cracked black pepper to taste

Instructions

1. Warm the oven to 375°F (190°C) and prepare the peppers. Clean the bell peppers and pat them dry. Cut off the tops and take out the seeds and membranes with care. Put the peppers in a baking dish so that they stand up straight. Drizzle olive oil over them. Add pepper and salt.
2. If you want to, cook the peppers: The peppers should be baked in a hot oven for 10 to 15 minutes or until they start to get a little soft. This makes them more tender and helps them cook faster in the steamer.
3. To make the stuffing, heat a large skillet over medium-low heat while you cook the peppers (if you want to). Break up the ground chicken with a spoon as you cook it until it turns brown. Get rid of any extra fat.
4. Add vegetables and aromatics. Put the onion, celery, and garlic in the pan and cook for three to four minutes until the vegetables are soft. The tomato paste, oregano, cumin, chili powder, salt, and pepper should all be mixed in now. Stir everything together for one more minute.
5. Add quinoa: Add the cooked quinoa and stir it in. Cook for one to two minutes, until it's fully heated through.
6. Put the chicken and quinoa mixture into the peppers. If you used pre-cooked peppers, take them out of the oven and carefully spoon the mixture into each pepper, making sure not to overfill them.
7. To steam the peppers, follow the directions on the package and fill your electric steamer with water. Then, bring it to a slow boil. Put the stuffed peppers in the steamer basket so that they stand up straight. Put the lid on top and steam for 20 to 25 minutes until the chicken is done and the peppers are soft. By sticking a knife into the thickest part of a pepper, you can tell if it's done. It should be easy to slide in.
8. If you want to, make the sauce: Put the crushed tomatoes, chicken broth, tomato paste, brown sugar, oregano, salt, and pepper in a saucepan. Let it sit while the peppers steam. Let it simmer for 10 to 15 minutes, stirring every now and then, until it gets a little thicker.
9. Put out: Carefully move the stuffed peppers from the steaming pan to the plates. You can drizzle the dish with the sauce and top it off with fresh parsley. Serve right away and enjoy!

83. CHICKEN AND CHORIZO SAUSAGE STEW

Prep Time: 15 minutes | Cook Time: 20-25 minutes

Total Time: 35-40 minutes | Servings: 4

Ingredients

- 1 cup of chicken broth
- 1 tbsp olive oil
- 1/2 pound chorizo sausage, sliced
- 1/4 tsp smoked paprika
- 1 green bell pepper, diced
- 1 red bell pepper, diced
- 1 medium onion, diced
- 1 (15 ounce) can black beans, rinsed and drained
- 1 tsp dried oregano
- 1 (14.5 ounce) can diced tomatoes, undrained
- 2 cloves garlic, minced
- 1/2 tsp ground cumin
- 1 pound boneless, skinless chicken breasts or thighs, cut into bite-sized pieces
- Salt and freshly cracked black pepper to taste
- Chopped fresh cilantro, for garnish

Instructions

1. Get the steamer ready: Follow the directions on the package to fill your electric steamer with water and bring it to a slow boil.
2. Warm up the oil in a pan. Set the olive oil in a large skillet or pan over medium heat while the water heats up.
3. Brown the chorizo and chicken. Put the chicken pieces and cook for 5-7 minutes, or until they are golden brown on all sides. Take the chicken out of the pan and set it aside. It will take about 3–4 minutes of cooking after adding the chorizo sausage until it starts to give off its fat.
4. Add the bell peppers, onion, and garlic to the pan with the chorizo and cook them until they are soft. Let the vegetables cook for 5 to 7 minutes, or until they get soft.
5. Mix the following in the pan: In a pan, mix the black beans, oregano, cumin, paprika, salt, and pepper. Then add the diced tomatoes. Mix everything together, then bring it to a simmer.
6. Put the chicken in the steamer. Put the browned chicken back to the pan and stir to coat in the sauce. Carefully move everything from the pan to a bowl or plate that can go in a steamer.
7. To steam the stew, put the bowl or plate with the stew in it in the steamer basket. Cover and steam for twenty to twenty-five minutes, or until the stew is hot and the chicken is cooked all the way through. To see if the chicken is done, stick a fork into the thickest part of a piece. It should be easy to flake.
8. To serve, carefully move the steamed Chicken and Chorizo Sausage Stew to bowls. You can add chopped fresh cilantro as a garnish and serve with rice or your favorite crusty bread.

84. POACHED CHICKEN SALAD

Prep Time: 10 minutes | Cook Time: 15-20 minutes

Total Time: 25-30 minutes | Servings: 2-3

Ingredients

For the Poached Chicken:

- 1 bay leaf
- 1 cup of water (or chicken broth for added flavor)
- 1/2 tsp dried thyme
- 1 boneless, skinless chicken breast (6-8 ounce)
- Salt and freshly cracked black pepper to taste

For the Salad:

- 1 tbsp Dijon mustard
- 2 tbsp mayonnaise (or plain yogurt for lighter option)
- 1/4 cup of chopped red onion
- 1/2 cup of chopped celery
- 1 tbsp chopped fresh herbs (parsley, dill, or chives)
- 1/4 cup of chopped green grapes
- Salt and freshly cracked black pepper to taste

Instructions

1. Get the steamer ready: Follow the directions on the package to fill your electric steamer with water (or chicken broth) and bring it to a low simmer. Add the bay leaf, salt, pepper, and thyme to the water for more flavor.
2. To poach the chicken, put the chicken breasts on a plate or bowl that can go in a steamer. Slowly put the plate or bowl in the steamer basket and cover it. Place the chicken in the steamer for 15-20 minutes or until it is fully cooked and the internal temperature reaches 165°F. A meat thermometer can be put into the thickest part of the breast to see if it's done.
3. Take the chicken off the heat and shred it. While the chicken is cooking, get the salad ingredients ready. After cooking, take the chicken out of the steamer and let it cool down a bit. You can use two forks or your fingers to shred the chicken. Throw away the bones and skin, if there are any.
4. Mix the salad ingredients: Put the chopped celery, red onion, grapes (if using), and shredded chicken in a bowl.
5. Prepare the sauce: Put yogurt, Dijon mustard, herbs, salt, and pepper in a separate small dish. Use a whisk to mix the ingredients together.
6. Put the salad together: Add as much dressing as you like to the chicken mixture and gently toss to coat. Change the seasonings to your liking.
7. Put out: You can eat the poached chicken salad by itself, in a sandwich on bread, or in a tortilla. If you want something lighter, you can serve it over lettuce leaves.

INTERNATIONAL DISHES

85. BRAZILIAN COXINHA CHICKEN CROQUETTES

Prep Time: 30 minutes | Cook Time: 20-25 minutes

Total Time: 55-60 minutes | Servings: 12-15

Ingredients

For the Filling:

- 1 (13.5 ounce) can cream of chicken soup
- 1/4 cup of chopped fresh parsley
- 1/4 tsp salt
- 1/4 tsp freshly cracked black pepper
- 1 onion, diced
- 2 cloves garlic, minced
- 1/2 tsp dried oregano
- 2 boneless, skinless chicken breasts, cooked and shredded
- 1 tbsp olive oil

For the Dough:

- 1 tsp salt
- 1/2 cup of vegetable oil
- 1 egg, beaten
- 4 cups of all-purpose flour
- 1 cup of milk
- 2 cups of water

For Steaming and Coating:

- 1 cup of panko breadcrumbs
- Cooking spray

Instructions

1. In a large saucepan, melt the butter over medium-low heat. Add the olive oil and stir it around. Put in the onion and cook for about 5 minutes, until it gets soft. Put the garlic and cook for one more minute.
2. Cream of chicken soup, parsley, oregano, salt, and pepper should be added. Add everything together and stir. Cook for about 5 minutes or until everything is hot and thick. Take it off the heat and let it cool down a bit.
3. Prepare the dough: Put water, milk, vegetable oil, and salt in a large pot. Heat it up and bring it to a boil. Take the pan off the heat and whisk in the flour slowly. Do this until a smooth dough forms. Make sure to stir the dough really well so it doesn't stick to the pot sides.
4. Move the dough to a surface that has been lightly floured. Work it out for five minutes or until it's smooth and springy. Put some plastic wrap over it and let it sit for 15 minutes.
5. To combine the coxinha, divide the dough into 12 to 15 equal pieces. Make a ball out of each piece and flatten it out. Put a tbsp of the cool filling in the middle of each dough ball.
6. To make a teardrop shape, pinch the edges of the dough together around the filling. Use your hands to flatten out the shape of each filled dough ball.
7. Follow the manufacturer's instructions for the coxinha and fill your electric steamer with water. Then, bring it to a slow boil. Spray cooking spray on the steamer basket just a little. Put the coxinhas together in the basket, leaving space between them.
8. Put the lid on top and steam for 20 to 25 minutes or until the dough is fully cooked and feels firm when touched.
9. To make the coating, wait for the coxinha to steam. Put panko breadcrumbs in a small bowl.
10. If you want to, coat the coxinha. Once the coxinhas are cooked, carefully dip each in the egg, then roll it in the panko breadcrumbs to cover it all. If you want to be healthier, you can skip this step.
11. Put out: When the steamed coxinha is ready, dip it in your favorite sauce, like aji sauce, ketchup, or mustard.

86. KOREAN MANDU DUMPLINGS WITH KIMCHI DIP

Prep Time: 30 minutes | Cook Time: 15-20 minutes

Total Time: 45-50 minutes | Servings: 4-6

Ingredients

For the Dumplings:

- 1/2 cup of chopped napa cabbage, finely shredded
- 1 package wonton wrappers (about 50 pieces)
- 1 tsp minced garlic
- 1 tbsp grated ginger
- 1/4 cup of chopped green onions
- 1 tbsp sesame oil
- 1 pound ground pork
- 1 tbsp soy sauce
- 1/4 tsp black pepper
- 1/2 tsp salt

For the Kimchi Dip:

- 1/4 cup of gochujang (Korean chili paste)
- 1/2 tsp grated ginger
- 2 tbsp soy sauce
- 1 tbsp rice vinegar
- 1/4 cup of chopped green onions
- 1 clove garlic, minced
- 1 tbsp sesame oil
- 1/2 cup of kimchi, finely chopped

Instructions

1. Get the filling ready. Put the ground pork, shredded cabbage, green onions, ginger, soy sauce, sesame oil, garlic, salt, and pepper in a large bowl. Mix the ingredients well until they are all mixed in.
2. Chop the kimchi and put it in a separate bowl. Add the gochujang, soy sauce, rice vinegar, sesame oil, ginger, garlic, and green onions. After mixing well, set it aside.
3. Put the dumplings together: A wonton wrapper should be laid on a flat surface. In the middle, put a tbsp of spread. To make the edges of the wrapper wet, brush them with water. To make a half-moon shape, fold the wrapper over the filling and pinch the edges together to seal them well. Do it again with the rest of the wrappers and filling.
4. To steam the dumplings, follow the directions on the package to fill your electric steamer with water and bring it to a slow boil. Line up the dumplings in your steamer basket so they are all in one layer. Leave some space between them. The dumplings are done when the filling is no longer pink, and the lid is back on. Steam for 15 to 20 minutes.
5. Serve: Move the steamed dumplings carefully to plates for serving. Serve hot with the kimchi dip that you've already made. This way, everyone can choose how spicy their dip is.

87. MOROCCAN CHICKEN MSEMEN WITH HONEY BUTTER

Prep Time: 30 minutes | Cook Time: 20-25 minutes

Total Time: 55-60 minutes | Servings: 4

Ingredients

For the Msemen Dough:

- 1 tbsp melted butter
- 1 tsp salt
- 1/2 cup of lukewarm water
- 1/4 cup of vegetable oil, for brushing
- 2 cups of all-purpose flour

For the Chicken Filling:

- 1/4 tsp black pepper
- 1/4 cup of chopped fresh cilantro
- 1 onion, diced
- 1/4 tsp ground cumin
- 1 tbsp olive oil
- 2 cloves garlic, minced
- 1 pound boneless, skinless chicken breasts, cooked and shredded
- 1/4 tsp cayenne pepper (optional)
- 1/2 tsp ground ginger
- 1/2 tsp ground turmeric
- 1/4 tsp salt

For the Honey Butter:

- 4 tbsp softened butter
- 1/4 tsp ground cinnamon
- 2 tbsp honey

Instructions

1. In a large dish, mix the salt and flour together to make the dough. Rub the melted butter with your fingertips until it's all mixed in. Slowly put the warm water and mix until a shaggy dough forms. Do not add more flour to the surface. For five minutes, work the dough until it is smooth and springy. Put a damp cloth over the dough and let it sit for 30 minutes.
2. Make the chicken filling. Put olive oil in a big skillet and heat it over medium-low heat while the dough rests. Put in the onion and cook for about 5 minutes, until it gets soft. Put the garlic and cook for one more minute.
3. Ginger, turmeric, cumin, cayenne pepper (if using), salt, and pepper should all be added now. Stir occasionally for 5 minutes, or until everything is hot and the flavors are mixed. Take it off the heat and add the chopped cilantro.
4. To put the Msemen together, divide the dough into 4 equal balls. Sprinkle some flour on a work surface and roll out each ball into an 8- to 10-inch-wide thin circle. Apply vegetable oil to the outside of each circle.
5. First, fold the circle in half. Then, fold it in half again to make a quarter-sized square. Again, use an oil brush to cover the top layer. Do the folding and layering process again, this time making an 8-layer square.

6. And then steam it. Roll out the square of layered dough into a thin circle that's about 12 to 14 inches across. Put the circle in the basket of your electric steamer. If you are steaming more than one at a time, leave space between them. Follow the directions on the package to fill the steamer with water and bring it to a slow boil.
7. Ten to twelve minutes of steam: Cover the Msemen and steam them until they are fully cooked and have a little puff to them.
8. Make the honey butter while the Msemen steam: Mix softened butter, honey, and cinnamon in a small bowl with a whisk until the mixture is smooth and creamy.
9. When ready to serve, carefully remove the Msemen from the steamer and brush them immediately with the honey butter. Cut the Msemen into squares or triangles, and then fill them with the chicken mixture. Serve them warm. Enjoy!

88. ITALIAN STEAMED MUSSELS WITH GARLIC

Prep Time: 10 minutes | Cook Time: 15-20 minutes

Total Time: 25-30 minutes | Servings: 2-3

Ingredients

- 2 pounds mussels, debearded and cleaned
- 2 cloves garlic, minced
- 1/4 tsp dried oregano
- 1 tbsp olive oil
- 1/4 cup of chopped fresh parsley
- 1/2 cup of dry white wine
- 1/4 tsp red pepper flakes (optional)
- Pinch of salt and freshly cracked black pepper to taste
- Crusty bread, for serving (optional)

Instructions

1. Get the mussels ready. Throw away anything that is broken or open. For extra clean shells, use a stiff brush to get rid of any sand or grit. Clams should be rinsed under cold running water and then drained.
2. Get the broth ready: To make the sauce, put white wine, oregano, red pepper flakes (if using), salt, parsley, and pepper in a bowl. Combine well.
3. Make the mussels steamy: Follow the directions on the package to fill your electric steamer with water and bring it to a slow boil. Put the mussels in the steamer basket so that they are all in one layer. Pour the broth that you made over the mussels.
4. Put the lid on the steamer and steam for 15 to 20 minutes, or until the mussels open and the shells are just barely open. Put away any mussels that haven't been opened yet; they might not be safe to eat.
5. To serve, carefully move the mussels with broth from the steaming pan to the bowls. Add extra fresh parsley if you want, and serve right away with crusty bread to dip in the tasty broth.

89. VIETNAMESE STEAMED BANH BEO RICE CAKES

Prep Time: 20 minutes | Cook Time: 20-25 minutes

Total Time: 40-45 minutes | Servings: 4-6

Ingredients

For the Rice Cakes:

- 1 cup of rice flour
- 1/2 tsp salt
- 1 cup of tapioca flour
- 4 cups of water (warm)

For the Shrimp Topping:

- 1 clove garlic, minced
- 1/2 cup of dried shrimp, soaked for 30 minutes
- 1/4 tsp fish sauce
- 1/4 tsp sugar
- 1 tbsp vegetable oil
- 1/4 cup of water
- 1 shallot, finely chopped
- Pinch of black pepper

For the Mung Bean Topping:

- 1 cup of water
- 1/2 cup of mung beans, rinsed and soaked for 2 hours
- 1/4 tsp salt

For the Pork Crackling (optional):

- 1 tbsp vegetable oil
- 1 small piece pork belly skin

For Serving:

- Chopped scallions
- Vietnamese dipping sauce

Instructions

1. In a big bowl, mix the salt, rice flour, and tapioca flour. This will yield rice cakes. Adding warm water little by little while whisking makes a smooth batter. Take 15 minutes to let the batter sit.
2. To make the shrimp topping, drain the shrimp and cut them into small pieces. Set a pan on medium heat and put oil. Cook until the shallot and garlic smell good. After you add the shrimp, cook for two to three minutes. Put in pepper, fish sauce, water, and sugar. Let it cook on low heat for 5 minutes or until the sauce gets thicker and the shrimp are done. Put away.
3. Soak the mung beans for a while, then drain and steam them for 20 to 25 minutes or until soft. Use a fork to mash the cooked mung beans, and then add salt to taste. Put away.
4. Mark the pork belly's skin with cuts and oil it. This will help you make pork crackling. Fry or grill them until they are crispy. Cut up into little pieces.

5. To steam the rice cakes, follow the directions on the package to fill your electric steamer with water and bring it to a slow boil. Grease the bowls or ramekins that fit in your steamer basket just a little. In each bowl, put about 2 tbsp of rice batter.
6. Let it steam for 10 minutes: Put the lid on top of the rice cakes and steam them for 10 minutes, or until they are set and fully cooked.
7. Put together and serve: Carefully remove the steamed rice cakes from the steamer. Put some mung bean and shrimp topping on top of each rice cake, and you can also add some chopped scallions if you want to. If you want, you can add pork crackling as a garnish. Serve right away with dipping sauce.

90. PERUVIAN STEAMED AJI DE GALLINA CHICKEN STEW

Prep Time: 20 minutes | Cook Time: 20-25 minutes

Total Time: 40-45 minutes | Servings: 4-6

Ingredients

- 1 tsp ground cumin
- 1/4 tsp smoked paprika
- 1/2 cup of chicken broth
- 1/4 cup of shredded Parmesan cheese
- 2 cloves garlic, minced
- 1/4 cup of chopped pecans or walnuts
- 1/2 yellow onion, diced
- 1/2 tsp ground turmeric
- 1 pound boneless, skinless chicken breasts or thighs, cut into bite-sized pieces
- 1 aji amarillo paste (3 tbsp) or 1/2 cup of roasted yellow bell peppers, blended
- 1 tbsp olive oil
- 1/4 cup of chopped fresh cilantro, divided
- 1/2 cup of evaporated milk
- Salt and freshly cracked black pepper to taste
- Cooked white rice, for serving

Instructions

1. Get the steamer ready: Follow the directions on the package to fill your electric steamer with water and bring it to a slow boil.
2. Get the oil hot and cook the chicken. Set olive oil on medium heat in a large pan. It will take about 5-7 minutes to cook after adding the chicken pieces until they are golden brown on all sides. Take the chicken out of the pan and set it aside.
3. Chop up the onion and garlic and put them in the pan. About 5 minutes of cooking will soften the food.

4. Put in the aji amarillo and spices: Add the cumin, turmeric, paprika, and half of the chopped cilantro. You can also use blended bell peppers instead of the aji amarillo paste. After one minute of cooking, the spices will start to smell good.
5. In the steamer, mix the following ingredients: Add the chopped pecans, chicken, evaporated milk, chicken broth, and sauteed vegetables to a bowl or plate that can go in a steamer. Add pepper and salt to taste.
6. To steam the stew, carefully put the bowl or plate with the stew in it into the steamer basket. Cover and steam for twenty to twenty-five minutes, or until the stew is hot and the chicken is cooked through. Stick a fork into the thickest part of a piece to see if the chicken is done. It should be easy to flake.
7. To serve, carefully move the Aji de Gallina Chicken Stew from the steamer to the bowls. Add the chopped cilantro to the top, and serve with cooked white rice.

91. GREEK STEAMED DOLMADAKIA GRAPE LEAVES

Prep Time: 45 minutes | Cook Time: 30-40 minutes

Total Time: 1 hour 15-20 minutes | Servings: 4-6

Ingredients

For the Grape Leaves:

- 1/2 cup of water
- 1 pound fresh grape leaves

For the Filling:

- 1/4 cup of finely chopped fresh dill
- 1 tbsp tomato paste
- 1/4 tsp freshly cracked black pepper
- 1/2 tsp ground cumin
- 1 yellow onion, finely chopped
- 1/4 cup of finely chopped fresh mint
- 1/2 cup of olive oil
- 1 cup of long-grain white rice, rinsed
- 2 cloves garlic, minced
- 1/4 tsp salt
- 1/2 cup of finely chopped fresh parsley
- 1/4 cup of chopped walnuts (optional)

For the Broth:

- 4 cups of vegetable broth
- 1/2 bay leaf
- 1 lemon, juiced

Instructions

Prepare the Grape Leaves:

1. If you use brined leaves, wash them well under cold running water. Put them in a bowl and add water to cover them. Soak them for at least 30 minutes or until they get soft and bendy. As it soaks, change the water once or twice.
2. Leaves that have been put in a jar should be drained and rinsed gently under cold running water. Use a paper towel to dry them.

Prepare the Filling:

1. Wash the rice and put it in a large bowl. Add the olive oil, onion, garlic, parsley, dill, mint, walnuts (if using), cumin, salt, and pepper. Combine well by mixing.

Assemble the Dolmadakia:

2. Place a grape leaf flat on a work surface so the vein side faces down. Put about a tsp of the filling close to where the leaf stem ends.
3. Fold the leaf's sides over the filling, and then roll the leaf up from the bottom to cover the filling completely. Do it again with the rest of the leaves and filling.

Steam the Dolmadakia:

1. Follow the directions on the package to fill your electric steamer with water and bring it to a slow boil. Fill the steamer basket with the dolmadakia that you've put together. Leave some space between each one.
2. Put the vegetable broth, lemon juice, and bay leaf in a different bowl. Mix the broth and water and pour it over the dolmadakia in the steamer basket.
3. Add the grape leaves and cover. Steam for 30-40 minutes until the rice is done and the leaves are soft. If you want to know if the rice is done, you can taste a filling.

Serve:

1. Move the steamed dolmadakia to a serving platter with care. If you want, you can drizzle the dish with more olive oil and lemon juice. You can serve it hot or cold.

92. MEXICAN STEAMED TAMALES WITH SALSA VERDE

Prep Time: 2 hours | Cook Time: 45-50 minutes

Total Time: 2 hours 45-50 minutes | Servings: 12-15

Ingredients

For the Masa Dough:

- 2 cups of masa harina
- 1 1/2 cups of warm water
- 1/4 cup of vegetable shortening, melte
- 1/2 tsp saltd

For the Pork Filling:

- 1/2 tsp dried oregano
- 1/4 tsp freshly cracked black pepper
- 1/4 tsp salt
- 1 tbsp chili powder
- 1 tsp ground cumin
- 1 (28 ounce) can crushed tomatoes
- 1 (14.5 ounce) can diced tomatoes, undrained
- 1 tbsp vegetable oil
- 1/2 yellow onion, diced
- 1 pound boneless, skinless pork shoulder, cut into bite-sized pieces
- 2 cloves garlic, minced

For the Salsa Verde:

- 2 Jalapenos, seeded and diced (adjust to your spice preference)
- 1/2 tsp salt
- 1/4 cup of water
- 1/4 cup of white onion, chopped
- 1 cup of tomatillos, husked and rinsed
- 1/2 cup of fresh cilantro
- 1 clove garlic

For Assembling and Steaming:

- Corn husks, soaked in warm water for at least 30 minutes
- Achiote oil (optional)

Instructions

Prepare the Masa Dough:

2. Put masa harina, warm water, and salt in a large bowl. Use a fork to mix the items together until a shaggy dough forms. For about 5 minutes, knead the dough until it is smooth and elastic after adding the melted vegetable shortening. Put a damp cloth over the dough and let it sit for 30 minutes.

Prepare the Pork Filling:

3. Put oil in a big pan and set it over medium heat. It will take about 5 minutes to cook after adding the pork until it is browned on all sides.
4. After adding the onion and garlic, it will take about 3 minutes to cook.
5. Chili powder, cumin, oregano, salt, and pepper should all be added along with the diced and crushed tomatoes. After 30 minutes, lower the heat and cover. The sauce should get thick, and the pork should be soft.

Prepare the Salsa Verde:

1. Put tomatillos, cilantro, onion, Jalapenos, garlic, and salt in a blender. Add water as needed to get the consistency you want and blend until smooth. Check the seasonings and make changes if needed.

Assemble and Steam the Tamales:

1. The wet corn husks should be drained and patted dry. Put about 2 tbsp of masa dough on the wider end of each husk to make a thin layer. Put a small amount of pork filling in the middle of the dough.
2. To completely cover the filling, fold the sides of the husk over it and then fold the bottom end up. Use kitchen twine or a strip of corn husk to tie the top of the husk closed.
3. Do it again with the rest of the dough and filling.
4. Optional: Brush the outside with achiote oil to make each tamale taste and look better.
5. Follow the directions on the package to fill your electric steamer with water and bring it to a slow boil. Place the tamales in your steamer basket so they are all in one layer, leaving space between them.
6. Put the lid on top and steam for 45 to 50 minutes until the dough is cooked and the filling is warm.

Serve:

1. Take the tamales out of the steamer carefully and let them cool a bit before serving.
2. Enjoy it while it's still warm with your homemade salsa verde.

93. GERMAN POTATO DUMPLINGS

Prep Time: 30 minutes | Cook Time: 20 minutes

Total Time: 50 minutes | Servings: 4-6

Ingredients

- 1/4 tsp nutmeg
- 6-8 tbsp butter
- 2 pounds Russet or Yukon Gold potatoes
- 2 eggs
- 2 tbsp cornstarch (additional)
- 1 tsp salt
- 1/2 cup of butter (optional, for garnish)
- 1 cup of cornstarch
- 1 tbsp fresh parsley (optional, for garnish)

Instructions

1. Wash the potatoes and cook them in a large pot of boiling water until they are soft enough to pierce with a fork. This should take about 20 to 25 minutes. Let it drain and cool down a bit.
2. Mash the potatoes: Mashing the potatoes well until they are smooth with a potato masher or ricer is recommended.
3. Put in the dry ingredients: Melt the butter and add the mashed potatoes. Season with nutmeg and salt. Combine well.
4. Knead the dough: Work the dough until it is smooth and stretchy after adding the eggs. If the dough is too sticky, add more cornstarch, one tbsp at a time, until it is easy to work with.
5. Make the dumplings: Wet your hands and cut the dough into 12 to 14 equal pieces. Form a ball out of each piece and then slightly flatten it into a disc. Leave them plain, or press your thumb into the middle to make a small hole.
6. Get the steamer ready: Follow the directions on the package to fill your electric steamer with water and bring it to a slow boil.
7. Pour the dumplings into the steamer basket, making sure there is some space between each one. Place the dumplings in a single layer. Put the lid on top and steam for 20 minutes, or until the dumplings float to the top and are fully cooked.
8. As the dumplings steam, you can melt butter in a pan over medium-low heat to make them brown. Slowly fry the dumplings one at a time until both sides are golden brown.
9. Serve: Put the steamed dumplings on plates for serving. Add melted butter and chopped fresh parsley on top (if you want to). Serve right away with your favorite German dish, like goulash, sauerkraut, or gravy.

94. JAPANESE GYOZA POTSTICKERS

Prep Time: 30 minutes | Cook Time: 20-25 minutes

Total Time: 55-60 minutes | Servings: 2-3

Ingredients

For the Gyoza Wrappers:

- 1/2 cup of warm water
- 1/2 tsp salt
- 1 cup of all-purpose flour

For the Gyoza Filling:

- 1 tsp sesame oil
- 1 tbsp soy sauce
- 1 tbsp grated ginger
- 1/4 cup of finely chopped green onions
- 1/4 tsp black pepper
- 1/2 pound ground pork
- 1/4 cup of finely chopped cabbage (Napa or regular)
- 1/2 tsp garlic powder
- 1 tbsp sake (optional)

For Cooking:

- Vegetable oil
- Water for steaming

For Dipping Sauce:

- 1/4 cup of soy sauce
- 1 tbsp toasted sesame oil
- 1/4 cup of rice vinegar
- 1 tbsp chili oil (optional)

Instructions

Prepare the Gyoza Wrappers:

1. Combine flour and salt in a large dish. Using a fork, slowly add warm water until a shaggy dough forms.
2. Knead the dough for five minutes on a surface that has been lightly dusted with flour, until it is smooth and elastic. Tent it with a wet cloth and wait 30 minutes.

Prepare the Gyoza Filling:

1. Put ground pork, cabbage, green onions, ginger, soy sauce, sesame oil, garlic powder, black pepper, and sake (if you want) in a bowl. Mix everything together well until it's all mixed in evenly.

Assemble the Gyoza:

2. Cover your work area with flour. Make 20 equal balls out of the dough. Make a thin circle out of each ball that is about 3 to 4 inches across.
3. Put a small amount of filling in the middle of each wrapper. To make the edges of the wrapper wet, brush them with water.
4. If you want to seal the package, fold it in half to make a half-moon shape, then pinch the edges together tightly. Check to see if there are any air holes. Do it again with the rest of the dough and filling.

Steam the Gyoza (Optional):

1. You can steam the gyoza in your electric steamer for 5 to 7 minutes before frying them if you want to. This step makes the filling softer and cuts down on the time it takes to fry.

Cook the Gyoza:

1. Set a big pan or griddle over medium heat. Spread out some vegetable oil.
2. Put the gyoza on each other, leaving some space between them. Fry on each side for two to three minutes, or until the bottom is golden brown and crispy.

Steam and Finish:

1. Add about a quarter cup of water slowly to the pan. Put the lid on top and steam for three to five minutes, or until the filling is done and the water is gone. This makes a tasty filling that is steamed and has a crunchy bottom.

Serve:

1. Place the cooked gyoza on a plate to serve. Add your favorite dipping sauce and chopped green onions on top (if you want). Enjoy!

95. CHINESE HAR GOW SHRIMP DUMPLINGS

Prep Time: 45 minutes | Cook Time: 10-12 minutes

Total Time: 55-60 minutes | Servings: 4-6

Ingredients

For the Dough:

- 1 cup of tapioca flour
- 2 cups of all-purpose flour
- 1/4 tsp salt
- 1/2 cup of warm water
- Vegetable oil for brushing

For the Shrimp Filling:

- 1 tbsp chopped scallions
- 1/2 pound (230g) peeled and deveined shrimp, chopped
- 1 tbsp soy sauce
- 1 tbsp chopped water chestnuts
- 1 tbsp minced ginger
- 1 tbsp rice wine vinegar
- 1/2 tsp sesame oil
- 1/4 tsp white pepper
- Pinch of salt

For Cooking:

- Water for steaming
- Optional garnishes: Chopped scallions, chili oil, ginger strips

Instructions

Prepare the Dough:

1. Put all-purpose flour, tapioca flour, and salt in a large bowl and mix them together. Add warm water slowly and mix with a fork until a shaggy dough forms.
2. Do not add any more flour to the surface. Knead the dough for ten minutes until it is smooth and springy. Put a damp cloth over it and wait 30 minutes.

Prepare the Shrimp Filling:

1. Chop the shrimp and put it in a bowl. Put the water chestnuts, scallions, ginger, rice wine vinegar, soy sauce, sesame oil, white pepper, and salt. After mixing well, set it aside.

Assemble the Har Gow:

1. Make 20 equal balls out of the dough. Make a thin circle out of each ball that is about 3 to 4 inches across.
2. In the middle of each wrapper, put a tsp of filling. To make the edges of the wrapper wet, brush them with water.
3. Make a half-moon shape with the edges of the wrapper by pinching and pleating them. Leave the top part open. Check to see if there are any air holes. Do it again with the rest of the dough and filling.

Steam the Har Gow:

1. Follow the directions on the package to fill your electric steamer with water and bring it to a slow boil.
2. Set the cooked harrow in your steamer basket, so it is all in one layer. Leave some space between each one. Put the lid on top and steam for 10 to 12 minutes or until the filling is done and the ground is clear.

Serve:

1. Move the cooked har gow carefully to plates for serving. Add chopped scallions, chili oil, and ginger strips as a garnish if you want to. Dip them in your favorite sauce, like soy sauce with a little vinegar and chili oil.

96. ETHIOPIAN MISIR WOT LENTIL STEW

Prep Time: 20 minutes | Cook Time: 40-45 minutes| Total Time: 60-65 minutes | Servings: 5

Ingredients

- 1/4 cup of chopped fresh cilantro
- 1/2 tsp turmeric powder
- 1/4 tsp salt
- 2 tbsp berbere spice mix
- 2 cloves garlic, minced
- 2 tbsp vegetable oil
- 1 (14.5 ounce) can diced tomatoes
- 1 tbsp grated ginger
- 1 cup of red lentils, rinsed
- 2 cups of vegetable broth
- 1 medium onion, finely chopped
- 1/4 tsp ground cumin

Optional Ingredients:

- 1/2 cup of chopped carrots
- 1 tbsp Niter Kibbeh
- 1 green bell pepper, diced

Instructions

1. Rinse and soak the lentils: Use a fine-mesh filter to clean the red lentils well. While you make the other things, soak them in warm water for at least 15 minutes.
2. Spices should be sauteed: On medium heat, warm up the vegetable oil in a large pot or pan that can steam. Put in the chopped onion and cook for about 5 minutes, until it gets soft. After adding garlic and ginger, cook for one more minute to let their smells out.
3. Put tomatoes and spices in it: Add the salt, turmeric powder, cumin, and berbere spice mix and mix well. Let the spices bloom for one more minute while you cook. Add the tomato chunks and their juices.
4. Mix the ingredients and steam: After letting the lentils soak, drain them and add them to the pot with the vegetable broth. Mix things well. Slowly bring to a boil.

Two Steaming Options:

1. Following the manufacturer's instructions, fill your electric steamer with water and bring it to a gentle boil. If your pot or pan is safe for steaming, you can use this method. Put the pot or pan with the stew that is simmering carefully right into the steamer basket. Put the lid on top and steam for 30 to 35 minutes, or until the lentils are soft and the stew gets thicker.
2. Pot-in-Pot Steaming: Put a heat-resistant bowl or steamer insert full of water inside the pot or pan where the stew is simmering. Put the lid on top of the pot and steam it for 40 to 45 minutes, or until the lentils are soft and the stew gets thicker. Every so often, check the bowl's water level and add more if needed.
3. Finish up and serve: When the lentils are done cooking and the stew has thickened, add the chopped cilantro and Niter Kibbeh, if you're using it. Check the seasonings and make changes as needed. Hot food can be served on injera bread or with cooked rice. Enjoy!

MAIN COURSES

97. STEAMED SALMON WITH LEMON & HERBS

Prep Time: 10 minutes | Cook Time: 15-20 minutes

Total Time: 25-30 minutes | Servings: 2

Ingredients

- 1/2 tsp salt
- 1/4 cup of fresh herbs
- 1 tbsp olive oil
- 1/2 lemon, thinly sliced
- 2 salmon fillets (6-8 ounces each), skin-on or skinless
- 1/4 tsp freshly cracked black pepper

Optional Ingredients:

- 1 tbsp white wine or dry sherry
- 1 garlic clove, thinly sliced
- 1/4 red onion, thinly sliced

Instructions

1. Prepare the salmon: Wet the fillets with paper towels and pat them dry. Put salt and pepper to taste, along with some olive oil.
2. Get the steamer ready: Follow the directions on the package to fill your electric steamer with water and bring it to a slow boil.
3. Put the flavors together: Put the lemon slices and herbs of your choice on top of the salmon fillets. You can also add the garlic and red onion slices here if you want to.
4. Cook the salmon in water: Make sure there is some space between the salmon fillets when you put them in the steamer basket. Steam the salmon with the lid on top for 15 to 20 minutes or until it's fully cooked and flaky.
5. Deglazing: You can make a simple sauce while the salmon is steaming by adding the white wine or sherry to the pan that the salmon was in with the cooking oil. Let it cook for a minute, and then scrape up any browned bits to make it a little less thick.
6. Put out: Place the cooked salmon on plates to serve. Pour on the pan sauce if you're using it. You can add extra fresh herbs and lemon slices as a garnish. Enjoy!

98. CHICKEN & CHORIZO SAUSAGE STEW

Prep Time: 15 minutes | Cook Time: 30-35 minutes

Total Time: 45-50 minutes | Servings: 4

Ingredients

- 1 tsp dried oregano
- 1/2 tsp smoked paprika
- 1/4 tsp salt
- 1 cup of chicken broth
- 1 tbsp olive oil
- 1 pound boneless, skinless chicken breasts or thighs, cut into bite-sized pieces
- 2 cloves garlic, minced
- 1/4 tsp freshly cracked black pepper
- 1/4 tsp cumin
- 1 (15 ounce) can cannellini beans, drained and rinsed
- 4 links mild or spicy chorizo sausage, sliced
- 1 red bell pepper, diced
- 1 jalapeno pepper, seeded and diced
- 1/2 yellow onion, diced
- 1 (14.5 ounce) can diced tomatoes, undrained
- Chopped fresh parsley, for garnish (optional)

Instructions

1. Get the steamer ready: Follow the directions on the package to fill your electric steamer with water and bring it to a slow boil.
2. Spices should be sauteed: Using a large pot or pan that can be used for steaming, warm up the olive oil over medium-low heat. After you add the onion, cook for about 5 minutes, or until it gets soft. After you add the garlic, bell pepper, and Jalapeno pepper, cook for one more minute so the flavors can come out.
3. Chorizo and chicken should be combined: If you add the chorizo sausage slices, cook for about 3 to 4 minutes, until they get a light brown color. Put the chicken pieces and cook until all sides are browned.
4. Mix the ingredients together and steam them. Take the diced tomatoes out of the water and add them to the pot with their juices. Add the chicken broth, oregano, paprika, cumin, salt, and pepper, and mix them in well. Bring to a low boil.
5. To steam the stew, carefully move the stew from the pot where it's cooking to the steamer basket. Steam for thirty to thirty-five minutes, or until the chicken is done and the vegetables are soft. There should be a lid on top. To see if the chicken is done, stick a fork into the thickest part of a piece. It should be easy to flake.
6. To serve, put the stew in bowls that have been heated through. You can add chopped fresh parsley as a garnish and serve with crusty bread or cooked rice.

99. STEAMED CHICKEN POT PIE FILLING

Prep Time: 15 minutes | Cook Time: 20-25 minutes

Total Time: 35-40 minutes | Servings: 4-6

Ingredients

For the Filling:

- 1 pound boneless, skinless chicken breasts or thighs
- 2 carrots, diced
- 1/2 cup of frozen corn
- 1 tbsp olive oil
- 1/4 tsp freshly cracked black pepper
- 1/4 tsp salt
- 1/2 cup of frozen peas
- 1 yellow onion, diced
- 1 tbsp cornstarch
- 2 celery stalks, diced
- 1 cup of chicken broth
- 2 cloves garlic, minced
- 1/2 tsp dried thyme
- 1 (14.5 ounce) can diced tomatoes, undrained

Optional Ingredients:

- 1/2 cup of chopped mushrooms
- 1/4 cup of chopped fresh parsley
- 1/4 tsp dried rosemary

Instructions

1. Get the steamer ready: Follow the directions on the package to fill your electric steamer with water and bring it to a slow boil.
2. In a large pot or pan that can also be used to steam, heat the olive oil over medium heat. This will help you saute the vegetables. Put in the onion, carrots, and celery. Cook for about 5 minutes, until the vegetables get soft. After you add the garlic, cook for one more minute to let its smell come out.
3. Get the chicken ready: Add the chicken pieces and cook until all sides are browned.
4. Mix the ingredients together and steam: Blend the corn, diced tomatoes with their juices, chicken broth, thyme, salt, and pepper together. Bring to a low boil.
5. To steam the filling, carefully add the mixture that is simmering to the steamer basket. The chicken should be fully cooked and the vegetables should be soft after 20 to 25 minutes of steaming. Stick a fork into the thickest part of a piece to see if the chicken is done. It should be easy to flake.
6. If you want to make the sauce thicker, you can add more cornstarch slurry (one tbsp of cornstarch mixed with one tbsp of water) to the pot after it has steamed and let it simmer for one more minute.
7. Move the steamed filling to a serving dish and serve. You can serve it as is or use it to fill homemade or store-bought puff pastry shells for a full pot pie experience. You can decorate it with chopped fresh parsley if you want to.

100. STEAMED SHRIMP & GRITS

Prep Time: 15 minutes | Cook Time: 20-25 minutes

Total Time: 35-40 minutes | Servings: 2-3

Ingredients

For the Grits:

- 1/4 tsp black pepper
- 1 tbsp butter
- 2 cups of chicken broth
- 1 cup of old-fashioned grits
- 1 cup of milk
- 1/2 tsp salt

For the Shrimp:

- 1/2 tsp Cajun seasoning
- 1/2 pound raw shrimp, peeled and deveined
- 1 clove garlic, minced
- 1 tbsp olive oil
- 1/4 tsp paprika
- Pinch of salt
- Pinch of black pepper

For Serving:

- Chopped fresh parsley (optional)
- Cajun hot sauce (optional)

Instructions

1. Get the steamer ready: Follow the directions on the package to fill your electric steamer with water and bring it to a slow boil.
2. Make the grits: Add the grits, chicken broth, milk, butter, salt, and pepper to a large saucepan. Over medium-low heat, bring to a boil. Next, turn down the heat to low. Let the grits simmer for 15 to 20 minutes, stirring every now and then, until they are thick and creamy.
3. To season the shrimp: Sprinkle the shrimp with salt, pepper, garlic, Cajun seasoning, and olive oil in a small bowl.
4. Steam the shrimp: Put the shrimp in a single layer in your steamer basket and set them aside while the grits cook. Cover the basket and put it over the water that is getting hot in the steamer. Steam the shrimp for 5 to 7 minutes, or until they are opaque and fully cooked.
5. Put together and serve: Put the cooked grits into two bowls to serve. Pour any pan juices left over from the shrimp steamer basket over each bowl and top with steamed shrimp. If you want, you can garnish with chopped fresh parsley and serve with Cajun hot sauce on the side.

101. LEMON GARLIC CHICKEN BREASTS

Prep Time: 10 minutes | Cook Time: 15-20 minutes

Total Time: 25-30 minutes | Servings: 2-3

Ingredients

- 1/4 tsp freshly cracked black pepper
- 1 tbsp freshly squeezed lemon juice
- 1 tsp lemon zest
- 2 cloves garlic, minced
- 2 boneless, skinless chicken breasts (6-8 ounce each)
- 1/4 tsp salt
- 1 tbsp olive oil
- 1/2 tsp dried oregano

Optional Ingredients:

- 1 sprig fresh rosemary
- 1/4 tsp dried thyme
- 1/4 cup of dry white wine or chicken broth

Instructions

1. Get the steamer ready: Follow the directions on the package to fill your electric steamer with water and bring it to a slow boil.
2. Marinate the chicken: Put the garlic, oregano, pepper, and salt in a bowl and mix them together. Add the lemon juice and zest. Brush the chicken breasts all over with the marinade after you put them in it. Let it sit for at least 10 minutes while the steamer gets hot.
3. Cook the chicken in water: Be careful when you put the chicken breasts that have been marinated in the steamer basket. For 15 to 20 minutes, or until the chicken is cooked all the way through and reaches 165°F (74°C) on the inside, cover and steam. An instant-read thermometer can be put into the thickest part of the chicken to see if it's done.
4. Choices of flavors: Before putting the chicken in the steamer basket, you can add more flavor by pouring the rest of the marinade into the bottom of the pan. It tastes even better if you put a quarter of a cup dry white wine to the bottom of the pan along with herbs like thyme or rosemary.
5. Put out: Place the cooked chicken breasts on plates to be served. If you want, you can drizzle it with any pan juices from the steamer basket. Serve with roasted vegetables, mashed potatoes, rice, or any other side you like.

102. SPICY BLACK BEAN BURGERS

Prep Time: 20 minutes | Cook Time: 20-25 minutes

Total Time: 40-45 minutes | Servings: 4-6

Ingredients

- 1 tbsp olive oil
- 1 tbsp chopped fresh cilantro
- 2 cloves garlic, minced
- 1 (15 ounce) can black beans, drained and rinsed
- 1/4 tsp salt
- 1/4 cup of finely chopped red onion
- 1 Jalapeno pepper, seeded and finely chopped
- 1 tbsp lime juice
- 1/2 tsp chili powder
- 1 tsp ground cumin
- 1/4 cup of rolled oats
- 1/4 tsp freshly cracked black pepper
- 1/4 cup of chopped green bell pepper
- 1/2 cup of cooked brown rice or quinoa
- 1/4 tsp smoked paprika

Instructions

1. Get the steamer ready: Follow the directions on the package to fill your electric steamer with water and bring it to a slow boil.
2. Mix the ingredients: With a fork, mash the black beans in a large bowl until they are barely chunky. Roll up some oats, red onion, green bell pepper, Jalapeno pepper, garlic, olive oil, lime juice, cilantro, cumin, chili powder, paprika, salt, and pepper. All of these things should be cooked first. Combine well by mixing.
3. Split the mixture into 4 to 6 equal parts to make the burgers. Make a firm patty out of each piece.
4. Line your steamer basket with the patties you just made to steam the burgers. Place the lid on top and steam for 15 to 20 minutes or until the burgers are fully cooked and browned.
5. Set a skillet over medium-low heat and put a little oil. If you want to pan-fry it, do that first. This will make the outside crispier. Carefully cook the burgers in a pan for two to three minutes on each side or until they turn golden brown.
6. Put your Spicy Black Bean Burgers on buns and top them with your favorite things, like vegan mayo, lettuce, tomato, avocado, or salsa.

103. STEAMED FISH WITH GINGER & SOY SAUCE

Prep Time: 10 minutes | Cook Time: 10-12 minutes

Total Time: 20-22 minutes | Servings: 2

Ingredients

- 1 tbsp rice wine vinegar
- 1 inch piece ginger, thinly julienned
- 1 scallion, thinly sliced (white and green parts)
- 1 whole fish (12-16 ounce), cleaned and scaled (choose a white fish like cod, snapper, or sea bass)
- 1 tbsp soy sauce
- 1 tbsp Shaoxing wine (optional)
- 1 tbsp sesame oil
- Pinch of salt
- Pinch of black pepper

Optional Ingredients:

- Steamed vegetables for serving
- Chopped cilantro for garnish
- Chili oil for dipping

Instructions

1. Get the steamer ready: Follow the directions on the package to fill your electric steamer with water and bring it to a slow boil.
2. Get the fish ready: If you want to cook the fish faster, you can make shallow diagonal cuts across the thickest part of its body. Use paper towels to dry the fish, then put it on a plate that can handle heat.
3. Put the sauce together: Put soy sauce, rice wine vinegar, sesame oil, ginger, scallions, salt, and pepper in a small bowl. If you want to use Shaoxing wine, add it now. Combine well.
4. Cook the fish in water: Spread the sauce out over the fish. Be careful when putting the fish plate in the steamer basket so that it doesn't touch the water. Place the lid on top and steam for 10 to 12 minutes, or until the fish is fully cooked and flaky.
5. Put out: Move the fish that has been steamed to a plate for serving. Add more chopped scallions and cilantro as a garnish if you want to. As a side dish, serve with chili oil and any steamed vegetables you like.

104. MOROCCAN CHICKPEA & SWEET POTATO TAGINE

Prep Time: 15 minutes | Cook Time: 30-35 minutes

Total Time: 45-50 minutes | Servings: 4-6

Ingredients:

- 1 tbsp olive oil
- 1 onion, diced
- 2 cloves garlic, minced
- 1 tsp ground cumin
- 1 tsp ground coriander
- 1/2 tsp turmeric
- 1/4 tsp ground ginger
- 1/4 tsp cinnamon
- 1 (14.5 ounce) can diced tomatoes, undrained
- 1 (15 ounce) can chickpeas, drained and rinsed
- 1 large sweet potato, peeled and diced (about 2 cups)
- 1 cup of vegetable broth
- 1/2 cup of raisins
- 1/4 cup of chopped fresh cilantro
- Pinch of cayenne pepper (optional)
- Salt and freshly cracked black pepper, to taste

Optional Ingredients:

- 1/4 cup of chopped fresh parsley
- 1 lemon, halved and thinly sliced
- 1/2 cup of chopped carrots
- 1/4 cup of sliced almonds, toasted

Instructions:

1. Get the steamer ready: Follow the directions on the package to fill your electric steamer with water and bring it to a slow boil.
2. Spices should be sauteed: A large pot or pan that can be used for steaming should be used to warm up the olive oil over medium-low heat. Put in the onion and cook for about 5 minutes, until it gets soft. Put ginger, garlic, cumin, coriander, turmeric, cayenne pepper (if using), and cinnamon. For one more minute, cook until the spices start to smell good.
3. Mix the ingredients and steam: Add the chickpeas, sweet potato, vegetable broth, raisins, and half of the cilantro. These should all be mixed. Add pepper and salt to taste. Bring to a low boil.
4. To steam the tagine, carefully move the simmering mixture to the steamer basket. Put the lid on top and steam for 30 to 35 minutes until the chickpeas are hot and the sweet potato is soft.
5. Add the last bit of cilantro and lemon slices if you're using them, and mix them in. Change the seasonings to your liking.
6. Put out: Put the Moroccan Chickpea and Sweet Potato Tagine in bowls to serve. You can top it with toasted almonds and serve it with couscous, rice, or crusty bread.

105. STUFFED PEPPERS WITH QUINOA & VEGGIES

Prep Time: 20 minutes | Cook Time: 30-35 minutes | Total Time: 50-55 minutes | Servings: 4

Ingredients

For the Peppers:

- 4 bell peppers
- 1 tbsp olive oil

For the Quinoa Filling:

- 1/2 cup of diced zucchini
- 1/2 cup of diced tomatoes
- 1 clove garlic, minced
- 1 cup of rinsed quinoa
- 1/4 tsp dried oregano
- 1/4 tsp cumin
- 1 1/2 cups of vegetable broth
- 1/4 cup of chopped fresh parsley
- 1/2 cup of chopped onion
- 1/4 cup of crumbled feta cheese (optional)
- Salt and freshly cracked black pepper, to taste

Optional Ingredients:

- 1/4 cup of chopped sun-dried tomatoes
- 1/4 cup of chopped fresh cilantro
- 1/4 cup of chopped mushrooms
- 1/4 cup of shredded mozzarella cheese

Instructions

1. To get the steamer ready, follow the manufacturer's instructions and fill your electric steamer with water. Then, bring it to a slow boil.
2. Prepare the peppers: Warm the oven up to 190°C (375°F). Please remove the seeds and membranes from the bell peppers and cut them in half lengthwise. Clean and dry with a towel. Use olive oil to coat the inside of each pepper half.
3. Put rinsed quinoa and vegetable broth in a saucepan to cook the quinoa. Put the lid on top and turn down the heat to low. Let it cook for 15 minutes. The quinoa should be fluffy and fully cooked by this time. Use a fork to fluff it up, then set it aside.
4. Warm up a skillet over medium-low heat and add a little olive oil. Put in the onion and cook for about 5 minutes, until it gets soft. Stir the food now and then for another 5 minutes after you add the garlic, zucchini, and tomatoes.
5. Get the filling ready. Put cooked quinoa, sauteed vegetables, crumbled feta cheese (if using), fresh parsley, oregano, cumin, salt, and pepper in a large bowl. Combine well.
6. Fill the peppers: Put an equal amount of the filling into each half of the pepper that has been prepared. Ensure the stuffed peppers don't touch each other as you put them upright in the steamer basket.
7. Cover the steamer and let it cook for 20 to 25 minutes, or until the peppers are soft and the filling is hot all the way through.

8. Put shredded mozzarella cheese on top of the stuffed peppers and put them back in the steamer for two to three minutes so the cheese melts. Serve: Your Electric Steamer Stuffed Peppers with Quinoa and Veggies are ready to eat aimmediately.

106. STEAMED PORK BUNS WITH HOISIN SAUCE

Prep Time: 30 minutes | Cook Time: 20 minutes

Total Time: 50 minutes | Servings: 12

Ingredients

For the Dough:

- 1 cup of all-purpose flour
- 1/2 tsp salt
- 1/4 cup of milk (warm)
- 1 tbsp sugar
- 1/4 cup of warm water (105°F/41°C)
- 1 tsp active dry yeast
- 1 tbsp cooking oil

For the Pork Filling:

- 1/4 tsp white pepper
- 1 tbsp oyster sauce
- 1 clove garlic, minced
- 1/4 cup of chopped onion
- 1 tbsp oil
- 1/2 pound ground pork
- 1/2 tsp sesame oil
- 1/4 tsp ground ginger
- 1 tbsp soy sauce
- 1 tsp rice vinegar
- Pinch of five-spice powder (optional)

For the Hoisin Sauce:

- 1 tbsp soy sauce
- 1 tsp sesame oil
- 1/4 cup of hoisin sauce
- 1 tbsp rice vinegar
- 1 tbsp water
- Chopped scallions (optional)

Instructions

Make the Dough:

1. Mix the sugar, flour, yeast, and salt in a large dish. Combine by stirring.
2. Using a whisk, mix warm milk, oil, and water in a different bowl.
3. Combine the wet and dry ingredients slowly while mixing them together until a shaggy dough forms.
4. The dough should be kneaded on a lightly floured surface for eight to ten minutes or until it is smooth and elastic.
5. Put the dough in a bowl with greased plastic wrap. It should rise in a warm place for an hour or until it gets twice as big.

Make the Pork Filling:

1. Put the oil in a pan and set it on medium heat. Put in the ground pork and cook it until it turns brown.
2. Put in the garlic and onion and cook for five minutes to make the food soft.
3. This dish needs soy sauce, oyster sauce, rice vinegar, sesame oil, ginger, white pepper, and five-spice powder, if you want to use it. Keep cooking for one more minute.
4. Leave the filling alone to cool a bit.

Assemble the Buns:

1. Flatten the dough with your hands and cut it into 12 equal pieces. Make a ball out of each piece.
2. Spread some flour on a surface and roll out each ball into a thin circle that is about 3 to 4 inches across.
3. Filling pork should be put in the middle of each circle.
4. To seal the dough around the filling, pinch the edges together. Make pleats all the way around the top of the bun.

Steam the Buns:

1. Follow the directions on the package to fill your electric steamer with water and bring it to a slow boil.
2. Leave some space between the buns when you put them in the steamer basket. Put the lid on top and steam for 15 to 20 minutes, or until the food is fully cooked.

Make the Hoisin Sauce:

1. Mix hoisin sauce, soy sauce, rice vinegar, water, and sesame oil in a small bowl with a whisk. Add chopped scallions as a garnish if you want to..

Serve:

1. Use the hoisin sauce to coat the steamed buns, then eat them.

107. KOREAN BULGOGI BEEF

Prep Time: 20 minutes | Cook Time: 20-25 minutes

Total Time: 40-45 minutes | Servings: 2-3

Ingredients

- 1/4 tsp toasted sesame seeds (for garnish)
- 2 tbsp brown sugar
- 1 tbsp rice vinegar
- 1 tbsp sesame oil
- 1 tbsp honey
- 1 tsp grated ginger
- 3 tbsp soy sauce
- 1/2 tsp black pepper
- 1 tbsp minced garlic
- 1 pound boneless, skinless beef flank steak, thinly sliced
- Green onions, thinly sliced (for garnish)

Optional Ingredients:

- 1/2 onion, thinly sliced
- 1 tbsp gochujang (Korean chili paste) for a spicy kick
- 1/2 cup of sliced mushrooms
- 1 tbsp Korean pear juice or apple juice

Instructions

1. Mix soy sauce, brown sugar, honey, garlic, sesame oil, rice vinegar, ginger, and black pepper in a large bowl to prepare the beef. Mix everything well. Toss the sliced beef in the sauce to make it cover everything. Put the meat in the fridge with the lid on for at least 30 minutes or up to overnight for a stronger flavor.
2. Get the steamer ready: Follow the directions on the package to fill your electric steamer with water and bring it to a slow boil.
3. Do not put more than one layer of marinated beef slices in the steamer basket. This is how you steam the beef. Cover and steam for 15-20 minutes until the middle is just a little pink and the outside is cooked. Look for doneness by sticking an instant-read thermometer into the beef's thickest part. The temperature inside should reach 145°F (63°C).
4. Set a skillet over medium-low heat and add a little oil. If you want to pan-fry it, do that first. This will make the outside crispier. Fry the steamed beef in a pan for a few seconds on each side until it turns golden brown.
5. Serve: Put the steamed Bulgogi beef on plates for serving. Put green onions and toasted sesame seeds on top. Try it with rice, lettuce wraps, or your favorite Korean foods like kimchi and pickled vegetables as a side dish.

108. STUFFED ACORN SQUASH WITH QUINOA

Prep Time: 15 minutes | Cook Time: 30-35 minutes | Total Time: 45-50 minutes | Servings: 4

Ingredients

For the Squash:

- 2 acorn squash
- 1 tbsp olive oil

For the Quinoa Filling:

- 1/4 cup of dried cranberries
- 1/4 tsp salt
- 1/2 tsp dried thyme
- 1/2 cup of chopped onion
- 1 1/2 cups of vegetable broth
- 1/4 tsp freshly cracked black pepper
- 1/4 cup of chopped fresh parsley
- 1 cup of rinsed quinoa
- 1 clove garlic, minced
- 1/4 cup of chopped pecans (optional)
- 1/2 cup of diced apple (optional)

Instructions

1. To get the steamer ready, follow the manufacturer's instructions and fill your electric steamer with water. Then, bring it to a slow boil.
2. Get the squash ready: Warm the oven up to 200°C/400°F. Clean the acorn squash and pat it dry. Cut each squash down the middle in half, and then remove the seeds and membranes. Spread olive oil on the inside of each squash half. Put half of the squash on a baking sheet so that the flesh side faces up.
3. Cook the quinoa: Do what it says on the package and cook it in a saucepan while the oven heats up. Rinse the quinoa and add it to the vegetable broth. Turn down the heat, cover, and wait 15 minutes after it starts to boil. The quinoa should be fluffy by this time. Use a fork to fluff it up, then set it aside.
4. Set a skillet over medium-low heat and put a little olive oil. Stir the quinoa while it cooks. Put in the onion and cook for about 5 minutes, until it gets soft. After you add the garlic, cook for one more minute to let its smell come out. You can add the apple dice and cook for another two to three minutes until the apple gets soft.
5. Mix the cooked quinoa, sauteed vegetables, dried cranberries, chopped pecans (if using), salt, pepper, fresh parsley, dried thyme, and dried cranberries in a large bowl. Combine well.
6. Stuff the squash: Put an equal amount of the filling into each half of the acorn squash that has been prepared. Place in an oven that has already been heated and bake for 15 to 20 minutes, or until the squash is soft and the filling is hot all the way through.
7. Broiling is optional. If you want the topping to be a little crispier, broil the stuffed squash for the last two to three minutes of baking. Be careful not to burn the filling.
8. Serve: Your Electric Steamer Stuffed Acorn Squash with Quinoa and Cranberries is ready to eat immediately.

DESSERTS & SWEET ENDINGS

109. STEAMED CHOCOLATE CHERRY BROWNIES

Prep Time: 15 minutes | Cook Time: 20-25 minutes

Total Time: 35-40 minutes | Servings: 6-8

Ingredients

- 1 cup of granulated sugar
- 1/2 tsp baking powder
- 1/2 cup of (1 stick) unsalted butter, melted and cooled slightly
- 1/2 cup of semisweet chocolate chips
- 1 cup of all-purpose flour
- 2 large eggs
- 1 tsp vanilla extract
- 1/3 cup of unsweetened cocoa powder
- 1/4 tsp salt
- 1/2 cup of pitted cherries, halved or chopped

Instructions

1. Get the steamer ready: Follow the directions on the package to fill your electric steamer with water and bring it to a slow boil.
2. Get the batter ready: When the butter melts, add the sugar and mix them together with a whisk in a large bowl. Adding the eggs one at a time and mixing them in is the next step.
3. Mix dry ingredients: In a different bowl, mix the cocoa powder, baking powder, salt, and flour together.
4. Add the dry ingredients: Slowly put the dry items into the wet ones and mix them until they are combined. Do not mix too much.
5. Cherry and chocolate should be mixed in. Incorporate the chocolate chips and chopped cherries using a spatula.
6. Put this in the steamer basket: Lightly grease a baking dish or ramekins that can handle heat and will fit in your steamer basket. You could also use parchment paper to line a steamer basket.
7. Pour the batter out: Put the brownie batter into the dish(es) that have been prepared. Use a spatula to make the top smooth.
8. To steam the brownies, put the dish(es) in the steamer basket and make sure there is room for the steam to move around. The dish is done after inserting a toothpick and pulling it out with wet crumbs. Cover and steam for 20-25 minutes.
9. Enjoy: Let the brownies cool for 5 to 10 minutes in the steamer basket before moving them to a wire rack to cool all the way down. As an extra touch, you can sprinkle powdered sugar on top. Serve with whipped cream or ice cream.

110. TROPICAL FRUIT STEAMED DUMPLINGS

Prep Time: 20 minutes | Cook Time: 15-20 minutes

Total Time: 35-40 minutes | Servings: 6-8

Ingredients

For the Dumplings:

- 1 tbsp vegetable oil
- 1/4 cup of water
- 1/4 cup of boiling water
- 1/4 cup of rice flour
- 1 cup of all-purpose flour
- Pinch of salt

For the Tropical Fruit Filling:

- 1/4 tsp ground ginger
- 1/2 cup of chopped papaya
- 2 tbsp brown sugar
- 1 cup of chopped mango
- 1 cup of chopped pineapple
- 1 tbsp lime juice
- 1 tbsp cornstarch
- 1/4 cup of chopped banana (optional)

For the Coconut Syrup:

- 1 tbsp cornstarch
- 1 can (13.5 ounce) coconut milk
- 1/4 cup of brown sugar
- 1/4 tsp vanilla extract

Instructions

1. Get the steamer ready: Follow the directions on the package to fill your electric steamer with water and bring it to a slow boil.
2. Get the dough ready: Put all-purpose flour, rice flour, salt, and 1 tbsp of vegetable oil in a large bowl and mix them together. Add the cold water slowly and mix until a shaggy dough forms. Turn on the stove and add the boiling water. Stir the dough really well until it comes together and forms a smooth ball. Put some flour on a surface and knead the dough for 5 minutes or until it starts to stretch. For 15 minutes, cover and let rest.
3. Get the filling ready: Chop the mango, pineapple, papaya, banana (if using), brown sugar, cornstarch, lime juice, and ginger and put them in a bowl. After mixing well, set it aside.
4. If you use a little flour, roll out the dough until it's about 1/8 inch thick. This will help you shape the dumplings. Cut circles out of the dough with a 3-inch round cookie cutter. Put some of the fruit filling in the middle of each circle.
5. Fold and seal the dumplings: Use water to wet the edges of the dough circles. To make a crescent shape, pinch and pleat the edges to close around the filling. Make sure the seal is tight so it doesn't leak while steaming.
6. There should be some space between each dumpling in the steamer basket so that they can steam. Put the lid on top and steam for 15 to 20 minutes, or until the dough is clear and the filling is cooked all the way through.

7. Set the coconut syrup aside while the dumplings steam. Mix the coconut milk, brown sugar, and cornstarch together in a saucepan over medium-low heat. With a whisk. Bring to a simmer and keep stirring the mixture as it cooks until it gets thicker and clearer. Now, take it off the heat and mix in the vanilla extract.
8. Put out: Pour warm coconut syrup over the steamed dumplings after putting them on a plate. Enjoy right away!

111. RASPBERRY AND ALMOND STEAMED CRUMBLE

Prep Time: 15 minutes | Cook Time: 20-25 minutes | Total Time: 35-40 minutes | Servings: 5

Ingredients

For the Crumble:

- 1/2 cup of rolled oats
- 1/4 tsp ground cinnamon
- 1/4 cup of all-purpose flour
- 2 tbsp cold unsalted butter, cubed
- 1/4 cup of brown sugar
- 1/4 cup of almond flour
- Pinch of salt

For the Raspberry Filling:

- 1 tbsp honey
- 1 tbsp cornstarch
- 1/4 tsp vanilla extract
- 2 cups of fresh raspberries
- 2 tbsp water

Instructions

1. Get the steamer ready: Follow the directions on the package to fill your electric steamer with water and bring it to a slow boil.
2. Rolling oats, all-purpose flour, brown sugar, cinnamon, salt, and cubed butter should all be mixed together in a large bowl to make the crumble. Rub the ingredients together with your fingertips until you get a crumbly mixture. Put away.
3. Prepare the raspberry filling: Put the raspberries, cornstarch, water, honey, and vanilla extract in a different bowl. Mix the berries in slowly so that they don't get crushed.
4. Layer in ramekins: Use a small baking dish that can be used for steaming to divide the raspberry mixture evenly between four ramekins. Cover all the berries on top of each serving with the crumble mixture.
5. Put the baking dish or ramekins in the steamer basket to steam the crumble. Close the lid and steam for 20 to 25 minutes, or until the crumble is golden brown and the raspberries start to boil.
6. Serve: Your Raspberry and Almond Steamed Crumble is ready to eat right away. You can put some vanilla ice cream or whipped cream on top if you'd like.

112. SPICED STEAMED PEARS WITH VANILLA SAUCE

Prep Time: 10 minutes | Cook Time: 20-25 minutes

Total Time: 30-35 minutes | Servings: 4

Ingredients

For the Pears:

- 1/4 tsp ground ginger
- 4 firm pears (like Bosc or Anjou)
- 1/4 cup of water
- 1/4 tsp ground cloves
- 2 tbsp honey
- 1 tbsp lemon juice
- 1/2 tsp ground cinnamon
- Pinch of nutmeg

For the Vanilla Sauce:

- 1/4 cup of sugar
- 1/2 vanilla bean, split and scraped
- 1 tbsp cornstarch
- 1/4 cup of heavy cream
- 1 cup of milk
- Pinch of salt

Instructions

1. Get the steamer ready: Follow the directions on the package to fill your electric steamer with water and bring it to a slow boil.
2. Get the pears ready: Don't cut off the stems when you peel the pears. Carefully cut out the core from the bottom of the pears using a melon baller or a small spoon. Don't damage the base.
3. Mix the spices together: Honey, lemon juice, cinnamon, ginger, cloves, and nutmeg should all be mixed together in a small bowl. Combine well.
4. Boil the pears: In your steamer basket, stand the pears up. Cover the pears with the spice mix. Put the lid on top and steam for 20-25 minutes until the pears are soft and a fork can go through them easily.
5. Put together the vanilla sauce: In a saucepan over medium heat, mix the milk, sugar, heavy cream, vanilla bean (or extract), and salt while the pears steam. Bring to a low boil and stir in the sugar while whisking.
6. Mix the cornstarch and 1 tbsp of cold milk in a small bowl. This will thicken the sauce. Carefully whisk the cornstarch mixture into the sauce that is already cooking until it gets a little thicker. Stir the food all the time for one more minute. Take the pan off the heat and throw away the vanilla bean pod if you used one.
7. Put out: Place the steamed pears on plates to serve. Add warm vanilla sauce on top and enjoy!

113. STEAMED BANANA BREAD WITH CHOCOLATE CHUNKS

Prep Time: 15 minutes | Cook Time: 30-35 minutes

Total Time: 45-50 minutes | Servings: 6-8

Ingredients

For the Banana Bread:

- 1/4 cup of packed light brown sugar
- 1/2 cup of melted unsalted butter
- 2 large eggs
- 1/2 cup of milk
- 2 tsp baking powder
- 1/4 tsp salt
- 1 1/2 cups of all-purpose flour
- 1/2 tsp baking soda
- 1/2 cup of granulated sugar
- 1/2 cup of semisweet chocolate chips
- 1 tsp vanilla extract
- 1 1/2 cups of mashed ripe bananas (about 3 bananas)

Optional Ingredients:

- 1/4 tsp ground cinnamon
- 1/4 tsp ground ginger
- 1/4 cup of chopped walnuts or pecans

Instructions

1. Get the steamer ready: Follow the directions on the package to fill your electric steamer with water and bring it to a slow boil.
2. Optional: Preheat the oven: If you want a slightly firmer crust, heat the oven to 350°F (175°C).
3. Mix dry ingredients together: Whisk the baking powder, salt, baking soda, light brown sugar, and flour together in a large bowl.
4. Mix the wet ingredients: Beat the eggs, milk, vanilla extract, and melted butter in a different bowl.
5. Mix the wet and dry ingredients : Slowly put the wet items to the dry ones and mix them together until they are just combined. Do not mix too much.
6. Add chocolate chunks. Next, add the chocolate chips and any other ingredients you want, like nuts and spices.
7. Get the pan ready: Coat a loaf pan or ramekins that can handle high temperatures with cooking spray. You could also use parchment paper to line a steamer basket.
8. Fill the pans with batter; fill the pans with batter. Use a spatula to make the top smooth.
9. To steam the banana bread, put the pan(s) in the steamer basket and make sure there is room for the steam to move around. If you stick a toothpick into the middle and it comes out with wet crumbs, the dish is done. Cover and steam for 30-35 minutes.
10. Baking is optional. Take the pan(s) out of the steamer after steaming and bake them in a preheated oven for 10 to 15 minutes for a slightly firmer crust and deeper color.
11. Keep it cool and enjoy: Let the banana bread cool in the pan for ten minutes. Then, move it to a wire rack to finish cooling. Cut it up and eat it plain or with your favorite spread.

114. STEAMED CHOCOLATE PEANUT BUTTER BARS

Prep Time: 15 minutes | Cook Time: 20-25 minutes

Total Time: 35-40 minutes | Servings: 8-10

Ingredients

For the Peanut Butter Base:

- 1/4 cup of unsweetened cocoa powder
- 1/2 cup of honey
- 1/4 cup of rolled oats
- 1 cup of natural peanut butter
- Pinch of salt

For the Chocolate Topping:

- 1/4 cup of plant-based milk
- 1/4 cup of honey
- 1/2 cup of unsweetened cocoa powder
- 1 tbsp coconut oil, melted
- Pinch of salt

Instructions

1. Get the steamer ready: Follow the directions on the package to fill your electric steamer with water and bring it to a slow boil.
2. Put together the peanut butter base: Put peanut butter, honey, rolled oats, cocoa powder, and salt in a large bowl. Mix well until you get a dough that is thick and sticky.
3. Put it in the pan: Put parchment paper inside a heat-safe baking dish or ramekins that can be used for steaming. Spread out the peanut butter mixture in the pan by pressing it down.
4. How to make the chocolate topping: Put cocoa powder, honey, milk, melted coconut oil, and salt in a different bowl. Use a whisk to mix the items until the mixture is smooth and a little runny.
5. Put the topping on: Carefully spread the chocolate topping out over the peanut butter base.
6. Put the pan(s) in the steamer basket to steam the bars. Put the lid on top and steam for 20 to 25 minutes until the chocolate topping is set and no longer runny.
7. As the bars cool, move them to a wire rack to cool completely. Leave them there for at least 30 minutes before cutting them. Cut it up into squares and enjoy!

115. STEAMED STICKY FIG PUDDING

Prep Time: 15 minutes | Cook Time: 40-45 minutes

Total Time: 55-60 minutes | Servings: 4-6

Ingredients

For the Pudding:

- 1 cup of self-raising flour
- 1/4 cup of milk
- 1 tbsp orange juice
- 1/4 cup of chopped dried figs
- 1/2 cup of butter, softened
- 1/2 cup of brown sugar
- 1 tsp baking soda
- 2 eggs, beaten
- Pinch of salt

For the Toffee Sauce:

- 1/4 cup of heavy cream
- 1/2 cup of brown sugar
- 1/4 tsp vanilla extract
- 1/2 cup of butter
- 2 tbsp golden syrup

Instructions

1. Get the steamer ready: Follow the directions on the package to fill your electric steamer with water and bring it to a slow boil.
2. Grease a bowl for pudding: Lightly grease a pudding bowl or ramekins that can handle heat and can be used for steaming.
3. To make the pudding, mix softened butter and brown sugar in a big bowl until the mixture is light and fluffy. Add the eggs one at a time and beat well. Then add the milk and mix well.
4. Mix dry ingredients together: Mix the flour, baking soda, and salt in a different bowl. Slowly put the dry ingredients into the wet ones and mix them together until they are just combined. Do not mix too much.
5. Figs and orange juice should be added. Chop the figs and add the orange juice.
6. Pour into the bowl: Pour the batter into the bowl or ramekins that have been prepared. Use a spatula to make the top smooth.
7. Fill your steamer basket with water and place the basins inside it. A toothpick stuck in the middle should come out with wet crumbs on it when the dish is done. Cover and steam for 40-45 minutes.
8. Set the brown sugar, butter, and golden syrup to melting in a saucepan over medium-low heat while the pudding cooks. Set the pot on low heat and add the heavy cream. Stir the sauce continuously for 5 minutes or until it gets a little thicker. Now, take it off the heat and mix in the vanilla extract.
9. To serve, flip the steamed pudding over onto plates and drizzle with warm toffee sauce. Enjoy right away!

116. GINGERBREAD PEAR STEAMED PUDDING

Prep Time: 15 minutes | Cook Time: 50-60 minutes

Total Time: 65-75 minutes | Servings: 6-8

Ingredients

For the Pudding:

- 1/2 cup of milk
- 1 1/2 cups of all-purpose flour
- 1 tsp ground cinnamon
- 1/2 cup of packed light brown sugar
- 1 tbsp molasses
- 1/2 tsp ground nutmeg
- 2 eggs, beaten
- 1/4 tsp baking soda
- 1 tsp ground ginger
- 1/4 cup of unsalted butter, softened
- 1/4 cup of chopped walnuts (optional)
- 1/4 cup of chopped dried pears (optional)
- Pinch of salt

For the Pear Topping:

- 1/2 tsp ground cinnamon
- 2 ripe pears, peeled and thinly sliced
- 1 tbsp brown sugar

For the Vanilla Sauce (optional):

- 1/2 vanilla bean, split and scraped
- 1/4 cup of heavy cream
- 1 cup of milk
- 1/4 cup of sugar
- 1 tbsp cornstarch
- Pinch of salt

Instructions

1. Get the steamer ready: Follow the directions on the package to fill your electric steamer with water and bring it to a slow boil.
2. Grease a bowl for pudding: Lightly grease a pudding bowl or ramekins that can handle heat and can be used for steaming.
3. Prepare the pudding: Softened butter and brown sugar should be mixed in a large bowl until the mixture is light and fluffy. Add the eggs one at a time and beat well. Then add the milk and mix well.
4. Mix dry ingredients together: Mix the flour, baking soda, spices, and salt in a different bowl using a whisk. Carefully put the dry ingredients into the wet ones and mix them until they are combined. Do not mix too much.
5. If you want, you can add nuts and pears. Add the chopped pears and walnuts (if using) and mix them in.
6. Prepare the pear topping by Putting the sliced pears in a small bowl and mixing them with the brown sugar and cinnamon.
7. Spread the pudding out: Put half of the batter into the pudding bowl that has been set up. Put the slices of pear on top. Cover the pears with the rest of the batter.
8. Fill your steamer basket with water and place the basins inside it. The dish is done when you stick a toothpick into the center, and it comes out with wet crumbs. Cover and steam for 50 to 60 minutes.
9. Vanilla sauce is optional: Iif you want to use it while the pudding is cooking. Mix the milk, heavy cream, sugar, vanilla bean (or extract), and salt in a saucepan over medium-low heat. Bring to a low boil and stir in the sugar while whisking. Mix cornstarch and one tbsp of cold water in a small bowl with a whisk. Carefully whisk the cornstarch mixture into the sauce that is already cooking until it gets a little thicker. Stir the food all the time for one more minute. Take the pan off the heat and throw away the vanilla bean pod if you used one.
10. Put out: Flip the steamed pudding over onto plates to serve. If you want, you can drizzle it with warm vanilla sauce.

117. STEAMED CHOCOLATE PUDDING CAKES

Prep Time: 10 minutes | Cook Time: 20-25 minutes

Total Time: 30-35 minutes | Servings: 4

Ingredients

- 1/2 cup of granulated sugar
- 1/2 cup of unsalted butter, melted and cooled slightly
- 1/4 tsp baking powder
- 1/4 cup of unsweetened cocoa powder
- 2 large eggs
- 1 tsp vanilla extract
- 1/2 cup of all-purpose flour
- Pinch of salt
- 1/2 cup of semisweet chocolate chips
- Optional toppings: Whipped cream, ice cream, chocolate sauce, powdered sugar

Instructions

1. Get the steamer ready: Follow the directions on the package to fill your electric steamer with water and bring it to a slow boil.
2. Optional: Preheat the oven: If you want a slightly firmer crust, heat the oven to 350°F (175°C).
3. Get the ramekins ready: Lightly grease four ramekins that can be used for steaming.
4. Get the batter ready: When the butter melts, add the sugar and mix them together with a whisk in a large bowl. Adding the eggs one at a time and mixing them in is the next step.
5. Put the dry ingredients together. Mix the baking powder, cocoa powder, salt, and flour in another bowl with a whisk. Slowly put the dry ingredients into the wet ones and mix them together until they are just combined. Do not mix too much.
6. Add the chocolate chips: Put the chocolate chips.
7. Divide the batter: Evenly pour the batter into the ramekins that have been prepared.
8. To steam the cakes, put the ramekins in the steamer basket and make sure there is room for the steam to move around. The dish is done when you stick a toothpick into the center, and it comes out with wet crumbs. Cover and steam for 20-25 minutes.
9. Baking is optional. After steaming, take the ramekins out of the steamer and bake them in a preheated oven for 5 to 10 minutes for a slightly firmer crust and deeper color.
10. Keep it cool and enjoy: Before turning the cakes out onto plates, let them cool in the ramekins for 5 to 10 minutes. You can put chocolate sauce, whipped cream, ice cream, powdered sugar, or any other topping you like on top.

118. STICKY TOFFEE STEAMED BUNS

Prep Time: 15 minutes | Cook Time: 20-25 minutes

Total Time: 35-40 minutes | Servings: 6-8

Ingredients

For the Steamed Buns:

- 1 tbsp vegetable oil, plus more for greasing
- 1/3 cup of warm water
- 1 tbsp unsalted butter, softened
- 1/4 tsp salt
- 1 tbsp white sugar
- 1 cup of all-purpose flour
- 1/4 cup of milk powder
- 1/2 tsp instant yeast

For the Sticky Toffee Filling:

- 2 tbsp heavy cream
- 1/4 tsp vanilla extract
- 1/4 cup of unsalted butter
- 1 tbsp golden syrup
- 1/4 cup of packed light brown sugar

Instructions:

1. Get the steamer ready: Follow the directions on the package to fill your electric steamer with water and bring it to a slow boil.
2. Get the dough ready: Mix the milk powder, sugar, flour, yeast, and salt in a large bowl with a whisk. Put the softened butter and mix it in until it looks like breadcrumbs.
3. Put in the wet ingredients: Mix the dry ingredients together while slowly adding the warm water and oil. Do this until a soft dough forms. Do not add more flour to the surface. Knead the dough for five minutes until it is smooth and springy.
4. First rise: Use greased plastic wrap to cover the dough in a bowl. Let it rise in a warm place for 30 minutes or until it goes double in size.
5. In a saucepan over medium-low temperature, mix the butter, brown sugar, and golden syrup. Warm them up while the dough rises. Raise the heat and cook, stirring all the time, for two minutes. Take it off the heat and add the vanilla extract and heavy cream. Do not stir. Put away.
6. To make the buns, punch down the dough and cut it into 6 to 8 equal pieces. Make a smooth ball out of each piece.
7. Put the dough balls on a lightly greased steamer basket, making sure there is space between them. This is the second rise. Put a lid on it and let it rise again for 15 minutes.
8. Before you steam the buns, put the steamer basket over the pot of boiling water. Steam for 20 to 25 minutes, or until the buns are fully cooked and slightly puffed.
9. Serve: Run the warm toffee sauce over the warm steamed buns and serve them hot. Enjoy!

119. STEAMED PUMPKIN SPICE CAKE WITH MAPLE GLAZE

Prep Time: 15 minutes | Cook Time: 30-35 minutes | Total Time: 45-50 minutes | Servings: 7

Ingredients

For the Cake:

- 1/4 tsp ground nutmeg
- 2 large eggs
- 1/2 cup of milk
- 1 cup of granulated sugar
- 1 1/2 cups of all-purpose flour
- 1/2 tsp ground ginger
- 1/4 tsp salt
- 1 tsp ground cinnamon
- 1 tsp baking soda
- 1 tsp baking powder
- 1 cup of canned pumpkin puree
- 1/2 cup of unsalted butter, softened

For the Maple Glaze:

- 1 tbsp milk
- 1/2 cup of powdered sugar
- 2 tbsp maple syrup

Instructions:

1. Follow the directions on the package to fill your electric steamer with water and bring it to a slow boil.
2. Optional: Preheat the oven: If you want a slightly firmer crust, heat the oven to 350°F.
3. Prepare a pan: Lightly grease a loaf pan or ramekins that can be used for steaming.
4. Mix dry ingredients together: Mix the baking powder, baking soda, flour, salt, and spices in a big bowl with a whisk.
5. Butter and sugar are whipped together in a different bowl until the butter and sugar are light and fluffy.
6. Add pumpkin puree and eggs. Add the eggs one at a time while beating the mixture, then stir in the pumpkin puree.
7. Mix the wet and dry items together by adding the dry ingredients and milk to the wet ingredients one at a time and mixing just until everything is combined. Do not mix too much.
8. Fill pans with batter: Fill the pans with batter. Use a spatula to make the top smooth.
9. Put the pan(s) in the steamer basket to steam the cake. The dish is done if you stick a toothpick into the middle and it comes out with wet crumbs. Cover and steam for 30-35 minutes.
10. Baking is optional. After steaming, take the pan(s) out of the steamer and bake them in a preheated oven for 10 to 15 minutes for a slightly firmer crust and deeper color.
11. After letting the cake cool in the pan for ten minutes, move it to a wire rack to cool completely. Then, glaze it.
12. For the glaze, mix powdered sugar, maple syrup, and milk in a small bowl with a whisk until the mixture is smooth. Spread the glaze over the cake that has been cooled. Put out: Cut your Steamed Pumpkin Spice Cake with Maple Glaze into pieces and enjoy!

120. STEAMED APPLE CRISP WITH OAT CRUMBLE

Prep Time: 15 minutes | Cook Time: 20-25 minutes

Total Time: 35-40 minutes | Servings: 4-6

Ingredients

For the Crumble:

- 2 tbsp cold unsalted butter, cubed
- 1/4 cup of brown sugar
- 1/2 cup of rolled oats
- 1/4 tsp ground cinnamon
- 1/4 cup of almond flour
- Pinch of salt

For the Apple Filling:

- 2-3 apples (like Honeycrisp, Granny Smith, or a mix), peeled and thinly sliced
- 1 tbsp honey
- 1 tbsp cornstarch
- 1/4 tsp vanilla extract
- 2 tbsp water

Instructions

1. Get the steamer ready: Follow the directions on the package to fill your electric steamer with water and bring it to a slow boil.
2. To make the crumble: Rolling oats, almond flour (or all-purpose flour), brown sugar, cubed butter, cinnamon, and salt should all be mixed together in a large bowl. Rub the ingredients together with your fingertips until you get a crumbly mixture. Put away.
3. Get the apple filling ready: Apple slices, cornstarch, water, honey, and vanilla extract should all be mixed together in a different bowl. To coat the apples without crushing them, mix slowly.
4. Layer in ramekins: Use a small baking dish that can be used for steaming to divide the apple mixture evenly between four ramekins. Cover all the apples on top of each serving with the crumble mixture.
5. To steam the crisp, put the baking dish or ramekins in the steamer basket. Top with the lid and steam for twenty to twenty-five minutes, or until the apples are soft and the crumble is golden brown.
6. Serve: Your Steamed Apple Crisp with Oat Crumble is ready to eat right away. You can put some vanilla ice cream or whipped cream on top if you'd like.

Printed in Great Britain
by Amazon